D1359859

AT OMA'S TABLE

AT OMA'S TABLE

❖

More than 100 Recipes and Remembrances
from a Jewish Family's Kitchen

DORIS SCHECHTER

HOME

A HOME BOOK

Published by the Penguin Group

Penguin Group (USA) Inc.

375 Hudson Street, New York, New York 10014, USA

Penguin Group (Canada), 90 Eglinton Avenue East, Suite 700, Toronto, Ontario M4P 2Y3, Canada (a division of Pearson Penguin Canada Inc.)

Penguin Books Ltd., 80 Strand, London WC2R 0RL, England

Penguin Group Ireland, 25 St. Stephen's Green, Dublin 2, Ireland (a division of Penguin Books Ltd.)

Penguin Group (Australia), 250 Camberwell Road, Camberwell, Victoria 3124, Australia
(a division of Pearson Australia Group Pty. Ltd.)

Penguin Books India Pvt. Ltd., 11 Community Centre, Panchsheel Park, New Delhi—110 017, India

Penguin Group (NZ), 67 Apollo Drive, Rosedale, North Shore 0745, Auckland, New Zealand (a division of Pearson New Zealand Ltd.)

Penguin Books (South Africa) (Pty.) Ltd., 24 Sturdee Avenue, Rosebank, Johannesburg 2196, South Africa

Penguin Books Ltd., Registered Offices: 80 Strand, London WC2R 0RL, England

While the author has made every effort to provide accurate telephone numbers and Internet addresses at the time of publication, neither the publisher nor the author assumes any responsibility for errors, or for changes that occur after publication. Further, the publisher does not have any control over and does not assume any responsibility for author or third-party websites or their content.

First edition: September 2007

Library of Congress Cataloging-in-Publication Data

Schechter, Doris.
    At Oma's table : more than 100 recipes and remembrances from a Jewish family's kitchen / Doris Schechter.
       p. cm.
    Includes index.
    ISBN-13: 978-1-55788-521-0
  1. Cookery, Jewish.   I. Title.
    TX724.S484 2007
    641.5'676—dc22

                                                                                    2007017776

PRINTED IN THE UNITED STATES OF AMERICA

10 9 8 7 6 5 4 3 2 1

PUBLISHER'S NOTE: The recipes contained in this book are to be followed exactly as written. The publisher is not responsible for your specific health or allergy needs that may require medical supervision. The publisher is not responsible for any adverse reactions to the recipes contained in this book.

Most Home books are available at special quantity discounts for bulk purchases for sales promotions, premiums, fund-raising, or educational use. Special books, or book excerpts, can also be created to fit specific needs. For details, write: Special Markets, Penguin Group (USA) Inc., 375 Hudson Street, New York, New York 10014.

*To the best grandchildren a
grandmother could ever have:*

*Matthew, Reuben, Sara, Ian,
Lila, Rachel, Molly, Edith,
Teddy, Noah, Sophie, Jeremy,
Aidan, Bradley, Alexandra,
and Emily.*

You are the future.

ACKNOWLEDGMENTS

◈

Of all the family and friends who have been so supportive of me over the years, the first person I want to thank is my husband, Marvin. You and our five wonderful children consistently helped me find and refine the cooking part of my life.

To my five children, Philip, Stuart, Laura, Renée, and Dena, whose different tastes honed my culinary skills over years of family dinners and wonderful celebrations. Thank you one and all.

To Hannah Kapit, who helped me believe in myself.

To Ruth Gruber, who made sure that the facts of my journey as a child to the United States were historically accurate—the only way facts can be.

To my literary agent, Carla Glasser, who trusted in me and provided me the opportunity to find my roots. Thank you, too, for introducing me to Evie Righter, who was an absolute joy to work with on every level. She understood who I was and am.

To Marian Lizzi, my editor at Penguin, who quietly and capably enabled me to revisit a past that I wanted to forget. I am very grateful for having taken the journey back. And to Katie, Marian's assistant, who was helpful to a fault in answering my questions about the the preparation of the manuscript.

To Zeva Oelbaum, who was so excited about this book and ready to participate in any way on its coming to light, thank you for your generosity and friendship.

To Luei B. Elsheik, with whom I have worked for years

at My Most Favorite Food, thank you for being such an enormous help with recipe-testing. And to Amilcar Palacios, also at My Most Favorite, thank you for working so conscientiously on the dessert recipes. To each of you, your assistance has been invaluable.

Which brings me to a very important group of family and friends whose participation in the preparation of the manuscript I could not have done without: my tasters. First, I want to thank the Austrian contingent, who were so crucial in verifying that the Austrian recipes were authentic: my cousin, Ruth; my friend Elisabeth; Rita from Indiana; and Andreas Launer of the Austrian Consulate in New York, and his wife, Eva.

In addition to the Austrian group are all the dear friends who came to the lunches and dinners, who shared in the spirited conversations and happy times as I wrote this book. Your reactions to the food of my formative years (and beyond) were instructive and insightful. Thanks to Lisa, Judy and Beth, Paul and Paula, Mark and Nancy (who introduced me to Elisabeth for which I am eternally grateful), Janice, Lonnie and Ross, Renée and Gerda (dear friends of Elisabeth's, each of whom shared her extraordinary past), Carla (again), Hannah (again), Zeva and John, Marty and Marsha, Denise, Graciela, Michal, and David.

It goes without saying that in the tasting department, I also owe special thanks to my children, my sons- and daughters-in-law, and my grandchildren, specifically Reuben, Edith, Rachel, Jeremy, and Teddy. When you get a thumbs-up for a recipe from a youngster with discerning tastes (and there are quite a few in this family!), you know you've got a winner.

Which brings me to the food itself: Thank you to Michael at Park East Kosher Butchers, Inc., for supplying me with some of the best cuts of meat I have ever tasted.

And to Scott, my son-in-law, for his support in our shared enterprise.

The writing of a book can be a solitary journey. This was not the case with *At Oma's Table.* Preparing the manuscript was an unforgettable experience for me. I am indebted and grateful to everyone who was involved.

CONTENTS

❖

AT
OMA'S
TABLE

INTRODUCTION

A FAMILY'S JOURNEY

Unlike some of my generation, I was fortunate to know one of my grandmothers, and I got to know her quite well. Her name was Leah Goldstein, and she was my mother's mother. Leah was born in Lemberg, also known as Lvov, which at that time was part of the Austro-Hungarian Empire, and would later become Poland. She had married Ludvig Goldstein, from Austria. They were the parents of four children; my mother, Berta, was the oldest.

My mother and my father, Efraim Blumenkranz, were married and living in Vienna when Hitler's army entered the city in 1938, shortly after I was born. The city was no longer safe for Jews, and my father, a determined man, decided that we should leave the city as soon as possible. After knocking futilely on the doors of one embassy after another, he finally secured a visa from the Italian government.

Oma and Opa, Leah and Ludvig Goldstein, in Vienna.

Years later, I learned from my mother that my father went to Italy ahead of us. When my mother and I arrived by train in Milan, we expected him to be waiting at the railroad station, but he was not there. We waited and waited until my mother found a taxi to take us to the address he had given her. We drove to Guardiagrele, to a small country town in the Abruzzi region of the province of Chianti. There, my father was waiting with open arms.

We lived in Italy from 1939 to 1944, as "free prisoners"—*librero confino*—an oxymoron meaning that we were allowed to walk around freely, though each morning my father had

My mother, Berta Blumenkranz, in Vienna.

to report to the mayor that we were present and accounted for.

We lived on the second floor of a two-family house with a yard. It was a happy time. My mother often told me that whenever she wanted to find me, I was always out in the fields picking flowers. I learned to speak both Italian and the regional dialect. (Although I was then no more than four or five years old, my parents had to ask me to translate!)

My father, Efraim Blumenkranz.

As a child in Guardiagrele, Italy.

My father and me in Italy.

One day, my mother bought a chicken. She fell so in love with it that she named it Dorrit, which was also my name. My mother built a box for the chicken and kept it on the balcony of our house. That chicken laid a single egg every day for me. When the chicken fell ill, my mother nursed it back to health and it followed her around the house, living a happy life.

While in Guardiagrele, I came to care about one of the kindest and unforgettable women I have ever met. Her name was Rosalia. I thought of her as a grandmother, and called her Nonna, even though she was seventeen, and single. Each day, she cooked and served lunch and dinner for her entire family. I would frequently go to her house for meals. Her warmth embraced me and has stayed with me to such an extent that I return to Italy every year. Long after the war, Rosalia told me that while we were in Guardiagrele she called me Maria when speaking to other people, to protect me from the Germans.

In July 1944 we were uprooted again, but this time we weren't fleeing. An invitation from President Franklin Delano Roosevelt had been issued for one thousand refugees to come to the United States as his guests. We were among those lucky enough to be chosen.

Traveling to America on the Army Troop Transport *Henry Gibbons* was a hazardous voyage. Thirty Nazi planes flew over us, and we were continually hunted by Nazi U-boats and submarines. By some miracle, our luck held and we were kept safe. We were part of a convoy of twenty-nine ships, thirteen of which were warships charged with protecting us from attack. Word came from President Roosevelt to the commanding office of the convoy, telling him that if we were attacked our refugee ship should be the first one protected.

The Henry Gibbons, *which brought us from Naples, Italy, to the United States.*

The ship was divided: We refugees slept on bunks in forward holds; in the stern were one thousand wounded soldiers, many of them with bandaged heads, arms, and legs, returning to hospitals in America. Escorting us on the voyage was a young, intrepid American official by the name of Ruth Gruber. Her job was to help us prepare for life in America.

Her 1st Hotdog

SOMETHING NEW . . . Here is six-year-old Dorrit Blumenkanz, who is among the 982 refugees from Europe who have found sanctuary at the Fort Ontario, N. Y., emergency shelter. The young lady is eating her first hotdog and she thinks it is quite tasty. Dorrit formerly lived in Vienna—before Hitler seized the city. International News Photo

My first brush with the American press.

At a special spring celebration held at Fort Ontario.

The soldiers overlooked the captain's order that there was to be no fraternization between them and the refugees. They would come to our part of the ship and bring candy and cookies to us children. I remember being seasick all day long. I was unable to keep my head up, and so I buried it in my mother's lap.

We arrived in America on August 3, 1944. On the very same day we were saved, Anne Frank was betrayed in Amsterdam. In Hungary, Adolf Eichmann was working ceaselessly to ship 750,000 Jews to death in Auschwitz.

We spent our first night in New York City on the ship. We were so excited to see the lights of Manhattan that most of us stayed awake all night. The next day we were transferred aboard a ferry boat, which took us to Hoboken, New Jersey, where a friendly newspaper photographer handed me a kosher hotdog and then took my picture. That photo ran in several newspapers.

From Hoboken we went by train to Oswego, New York, a small northern town between Syracuse and Rochester. We were immediately housed in barracks at a famous army camp named Fort Ontario, which had been transformed into an emergency refugee shelter. We stayed there for eighteen months, during which time I went to first grade and started to learn English. My mother was busy with my baby sister, and my father was given chores, including shoveling coal into our building's furnace. Adults needed a pass to leave the gates and enter town for six hours at a time. But the schools opened their arms to us children, and the older ones were permitted to stay in the library even after school hours.

One day my father, longing to see his relatives in New York City, found a way to leave the shelter. After meeting all his cousins, he returned to Oswego and told us he had fallen in love with New York, and that he was eagerly looking forward to our beginning a new life in America.

A few days later, he fell ill and was rushed to a hospital in Syracuse. The diagnosis was spinal meningitis, and he died within twenty-four hours. Our whole world collapsed.

My mother, Berta Blumenkranz, with my sister, Ruth, at Fort Ontario our first home in America.

Our last weeks in the shelter were filled with panic. Most of the government agencies demanded that we fulfill the promise we had made to return to our countries of origin as soon as the war was over. We soon learned, however, that a group of prominent people, including Eleanor Roosevelt, Secretary of the Interior Harold L. Ickes, and Ruth Gruber, the American official who had helped us aboard the *Henry Gibbons*, succeeded in influencing President Harry S. Truman to reverse the promise made to the late President Roosevelt. He made the announcement over the radio on December 22, 1945. The camp erupted in joy.

Seventy communities opened their doors to us, helping us find new homes, schools, and jobs for our parents. My mother, my sister, and I were allowed to settle in New York City because we had relatives there.

Our first home was an apartment in the Bronx, which we shared with my mother's sister, Ciel, a real beauty, and her husband, Rudy, but it was so small that we left and moved to the Lower East Side. At the same time, my mother's mother, Leah, whom we called Oma (grandmother in German) arrived from Europe alone. She had escaped from Austria and survived by hiding in Belgium, but her

My aunt Ciel, as a bathing suit model.

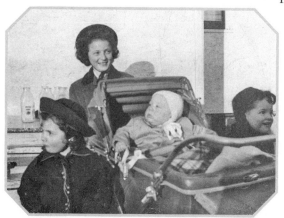

With Ruth and Freddy in Rego Park, Queens.

husband, her son, Yoschi, and her daughter, Regina, had all been killed.

Leah was living with us when my aunt, Ciel, gave birth to a baby boy, Freddy. A family decision was made: Ciel and Rudy would buy a house, and we would again all live together. We shared our first house in Rego Park, Queens, then we moved into another house nearby. My grandmother took care of the children while the adults went to work. I went to school, where a wonderful teacher helped me perfect my English and all the other subjects, all with deep understanding of what I had lived through.

Both my grandmother and my mother were business-women. In pre-war Vienna, my grandmother had worked in a shoe store owned by her family, while my mother, who had gone to business school, helped women select their clothing in an upscale boutique called *Modenpalais Julius Krupnik Wien, Toiletten fur die Dame* (Modern Palace Julius Krupnick, Vienna, Couture for Ladies). Like her sister, my mother was a beautiful woman, graceful and elegant with a soft voice.

Oma, in her sixties, soon became head of the house-hold. She shopped and cooked every day, and would walk to the various markets, traveling a route that took her to the kosher butcher, the A&P on Union Turnpike, the bakery, and wherever else she needed to go. The distances were far. After returning home, she would start to cook.

Every night, unfailingly, we would sit down at six o'clock sharp at the table I had set. The meals were simple, everyday fare: stews, or "potted" meat as my mother liked to call it, goulashes, brisket, boiled potatoes, and sturdy soups. The food was nourishing, carried over from what Oma had cooked in Vienna. There was always just enough, with nothing extra. Everything was made for that day. After dinner, I cleared the table and washed and dried the dishes. When my sister, Ruth, got older, she helped. In a world that was new to all of us, mealtime was predictable, the company dependable. I cannot say, however, that it was joyful or fun. Too much had happened during the war and the Holocaust. It was difficult for the adults to voice their feelings.

One topic of conversation I remember the adults did bring up was Vienna. My mother, in particular, enjoyed recalling her happy times there. To my young ears, life in Vienna seemed to radiate a golden glow. In turn, I had my own memories—of dear Rosalia and the times we shared in Italy around her lively and happy table.

A photo of me as a schoolgirl living in Queens, New York.

Several years later, as a student at the Fashion Institute of Technology in Manhattan, I met a handsome fellow student named Marvin Schechter. I was eighteen, he was twenty-four, and three months later we were married. By the time I was twenty-one, Marvin and I had three children—two boys and one girl—and we were living in a small house in Bayside, Queens. It was there that I began to live out my fantasy of what life could be like when a family gathered together to share food and celebrate important occasions. These included all the Jewish holidays, bar mitzvahs, bat mitzvahs, birthdays, weddings, and anniversaries.

Then it was on to a beautiful, big house in King's Point, Long Island, by which time we had five wonderful

My future looks bright.

children—Philip, Stuart, Laura, Renée, and Dena—and the house was always filled. I wanted to educate my loved ones about the events that mattered. It was my way of satisfying a closely held childhood dream.

It was in the 1980s that a friend of mine, Fred Schwartz, who was involved with the State Museum in Albany, told me that he had encountered a wonderful woman whom he thought I should meet as well. He added, "She brought you to the United States." I resisted his suggestion, but my daughter Laura, who has always been very interested in history, called her to ask if we might schedule a meeting. "I'd be delighted," she replied. At that time my restaurant, My Most Favorite Dessert Company, was located on Madison Avenue. The meeting took place there. The person whom my mother, my sister, Ruth, my daughter Laura, and I had the pleasure of meeting that *wonderful* day was Ruth Gruber.

It was as if we had always known each other. She and I bonded immediately, and that meeting has forever changed my life. Ruth Gruber is the most nurturing, most compassionate, most understanding woman I have ever met. Her professional accomplishments over the years are only part of her extraordinary story. Her ability to read the human heart rivals her remarkable résumé. Not long after we met, Ruth invited me to her apartment to look at photos of the journey we shared on board the *Henry Gibbons*, including pictures of the emergency refugee shelter in Oswego. The photographs were difficult for me to look at. Ruth allowed me to grieve, not once invading the privacy of my feelings. She became my surrogate mother. For me, she is an example of how to live. For more than twenty years now, I have been blessed with that good fortune. Whatever my endeavor, Ruth has always been there to encourage me.

My life with food began in New York City in the early 1980s, when I went from restaurant to restaurant selling cakes I had baked. That endeavor evolved into a bakery, My Most Favorite Dessert Company, in Great Neck, New York. From there I moved into a larger space in Manhattan, a restaurant on Madison Avenue near Eighty-Sixth Street, where I served breakfast, lunch, and dinner. In the early 1990s, My Most Favorite Dessert Company opened on Forty-Fifth Street between Sixth Avenue and Broadway, in the heart of the Theater District, where it now includes a bakery, a restaurant, a café, and a catering company, *and* a new name as well: My Most Favorite Food.

Writing this book has reconnected me to the lives that my grandmother and mother lived in the once-magical city of Vienna before the war and the Holocaust. It has also realigned me to my heritage, especially to the strong women in my family: Oma, my mother, my sister, and my aunt, Ciel. This book has given me unexpected joy as well as new strength to reawaken the recipes I have learned and to pass them on to my children, my sixteen grandchildren, and, dear reader, to you. I hope they help stir memories—and cherished family meals—for you and yours, as they have for me.

A Grandmother's Will

There was so much I didn't know about Oma's life when I was a child living under one roof with her, my mother, and my aunt and uncle. I thought she was beautiful: She was petite, with a nice figure. Her eyes were a soft hazel color. She wore no makeup, ever. She dressed simply, but with style, and was elegant in that unannounced European kind of way. She stood out not because of the garnet-and-ruby earrings or her sparkly necklace she sometimes wore when she dressed to go to a party, but because of her posture. Her carriage was remarkable, her back ramrod straight. Dignified people, I later learned, carried themselves that way.

She was of the old school. Respect was everything. Manners were of the utmost importance. In her opinion—and she was highly opinionated—there was a proper way to do everything, and you were expected to behave that way. She was fair, but strict. Family came first, and in her book nothing family-related ever went beyond the confines of one's own walls. This code of behavior was self-imposed, but it applied to her children and grandchildren as well.

What impacted my grandmother's life and so many other lives in Europe at that time was the chaos of the war. Up until those fateful days, Leah Goldstein had been living a very comfortable life in Vienna. She loved her handsome husband, Ludvig. In addition to being a devoted mother of four, Leah was also a businesswoman; she and her husband owned a shoe store. It was assumed that the future would simply continue to unfold as it had, happily, favorably. Why wouldn't it? They were together, living in a beautiful city. Vienna surrounded them with its magnificent parks and museums and restaurants and stores. They had friends. Family lived nearby. Life was good; it could only get better.

Then the war broke out.

By the time Oma arrived in the United States in 1945, she had lost her half of her immediate family, her homeland, and her home. Her beloved son, Yoschi, her darling daughter, Regina, and her devoted husband had all been picked up by the Gestapo in Belgium and taken to a concentration camp. She managed to survive the war by working in Belgium in an old-age home. She had endured an unbelievable amount of emotional suffering. What Leah found in the United States was what remained of her life: her surviving two daughters, a son-in-law, two granddaughters—my sister and I—and in time, a grandson. Everything else was gone.

Oma did not talk about her losses. She was stoic. In fact, I don't remember her talking about Vienna at all, except in the context of her never expecting to leave the city she loved. Why would anyone leave Vienna? she would ask. My mother was the one who liked to reminisce about the good life there. Those memories were a source of happiness for her, and for me, too. And little wonder, to my young ears, it all sounded grand. My relatives, on both my mother's and my father's sides, had enjoyed happy times there. Stories abounded of family reunions, parties with cousins and aunts and uncles and grandparents, wonderful food, laughter and light. My mother's memories made me dream. In time, I would try to re-create those memories of hers, with my own family, in my own way.

What Oma lost she would never again find. And so, with half her life over, she devoted herself to helping her

Oma Leah Goldstein.

daughters build lives in a new country. Oma bravely started over again. Her pleasures were quiet ones. When I was a young girl, she would take me to Radio City Music Hall, and we would have a good time. She saw to it that her daughters did prevail. She instilled in her granddaughters the importance of dignity, respect, perseverance, and independence.

She aged as she had lived—gracefully—and died at ninety-one.

She made an indelible impression on me. She was a woman of valor.

The Oma Way

This book is a collection of recipes: my grandmother's, as I remember them; my mother's, as I remember them, and my own, as I cook them. Leah Goldstein, my grandmother, kept no written record of her recipes, although in her later years I had the pleasure of having her visit our home on Long Island, where we would cook together, her showing me just how she had liked to prepare a goulash, for instance, and my telling her how I might adjust it to our tastes and the times. That said, Oma, a most practical and exacting women—the word taskmaster comes to mind, but in the gentlest, most soft-spoken of ways—did not deviate when it came to the following:

- She observed the dietary laws (for a brief explanation of the laws, see page 33).
- She shopped daily, which meant that our food was fresh.
- She always bought kosher meat.
- She used flavorless vegetable oil for cooking.
- She drank only tea, Swee-Touch-Nee, brewed from a tea bag. (The bags came in a red tin with gold accents, which always struck me as a bit showy for a person as self-effacing as Oma.)
- She allowed no junk food—no candy, no soda, no treats—ever.
- Last but not least, she wore sensible shoes.

Oma ran a careful household, and those of us who were part of it—with the exception of my cousin Freddy who got away with more than my sister or I even dared dream of!—knew the rules and respected them.

My mother was an infrequent cook because she worked—into her early eighties! The handful of dishes she made are memorable and appear in this book as well—among them, her legendary gefilte fish, her "potted" meats, and her unforgettable pound cake.

Where my cooking differs from Oma's is in the details. I tend to use lots of fresh herbs. Oma did not. I will also buy the occasional superb cut of meat, a standing rib roast or the veal roast on page 95. Oma would not. If I am in the mood, I will also use extra-virgin olive oil in place of flavorless vegetable oil to dress a salad. Aside from those few considerations, I share Oma's criteria when it comes to food preparation.

Whether you are making a recipe that was created by Oma, Berta, or me, you will need no special equipment or cookware. Oma did not use even a food processor. I do use one, but if you'd rather, do as Oma did, and chop the ingredients by hand.

About the Tastings

To test the recipes in this book, I created menus with multiple courses, ranging from appetizer to dessert. Most of the menus were for dinners, although there were one or two luncheons. An investigation into Liptauer (see page 25), one of my most favorite food memories, necessitated our departing from the traditional menu format. Instead of a traditional menu per se, I paired different versions of Liptauer with a selection of desserts, because all the dishes included dairy. And what a tasting that turned out to be! Our exploration of what was (and what could be) Liptauer became more animated with each variation, and I am happy to say we finally did arrive at just the right combination, replicating almost perfectly the one I remember from Oma's table.

The tasters at these enjoyable gatherings included a wonderful group of relatives and friends. Many of them have direct ties to Austria, and some to Vienna itself. Ruth Clapper, my father's first cousin's daughter, was born in Vienna and has memories of the occasions hosted by her grandmother, the renowned cook and my father's aunt, Chai Perl; Rita Grunwald, a dear friend who now lives in Indianapolis, was also born in Vienna, and has a fervent interest in fine music as well as food. Lisa Walborsky, a dear friend of Hungarian heritage, shed still more light on the Liptauer mystery, from a Hungarian point of view. And then there was a new Austrian friend, Elisabeth Pozzi-Thanner, who, although she professes to do little cooking now, did a lot of cooking in the past and is more knowledgeable about Austrian food than anyone I have ever met. She is also a remarkable human being and an oral historian by profession. Daughters, sons, grandchildren, cousins, new friends, old friends, all were part of the mix.

Over the course of the times we met, we shared memories, and stories. Rita spoke of her time as a child in Cuba—her family had fled Vienna as well. Ruth had memories of living in Bolivia, South America, where she and her family had lived before coming to the United States. There was a remarkable Austrian-born woman by the name of Renée, who recounted some of her experiences in the Resistance in France when she was a sixteen-year-old girl. Food brought us together, and as we told our stories and tasted the recipes in this book together, we honored our common bond.

A selection of some of the menus we shared begins on page 227. Following that grouping are menus for the Jewish holidays, including our singular Liptauer cum Dessert Tasting, which I mentioned above, prepared for Shavuous. May the menu you prepare, whether everyday or holiday, be memorable. Better still, may the experience of coming together for a meal with family and friends be as meaningful for you as it has been for me.

APPETIZERS, EGGS, AND SOUPS AND BREADS

APPETIZERS ❖ 19

Chopped Herring Salad ❖ Chopped Liver ❖ Gefilte Fish ❖ Liptauer (Fancy) ❖
Liptauer with Anchovies ❖ Liptauer with (More) Anchovies ❖
My Most Favorite "Liptauer"

EGGS ❖ 31

Deviled Eggs ❖ Eggs with Sautéed Onions ❖ My Mother's Omelet with
French Fries ❖ Vegetable Frittata

SOUPS ❖ 39

Chicken Soup ❖ Matzo Balls ❖ Matzo Brei ❖ Matzo Coffee ❖ Beef Broth ❖ Borscht
❖ Vegetable Broth ❖ Sweet-and-Sour Tomato-Cabbage Soup ❖ Vegetable Soup

BREADS ❖ 57

Challah ❖ Corn Bread ❖ Homemade Bread Crumbs ❖ Toasted Homemade
Bread Crumbs

APPETIZERS

Chopped Herring Salad

2 cups chopped jarred matjes
herring pickled in wine,
drained

1½ cups chopped, peeled boiled
beets (2 large)

1 cup chopped, peeled boiled
potato (1 large)

1 cup diced peeled apple (1 large)

½ cup diced onion (1 small)

2 tablespoons chopped sour
pickles

2 tablespoons white vinegar

1½ tablespoons sugar

½ teaspoon Dijon mustard

My Austrian friend Elisabeth Pozzi-Thanner tells me that chopped herring is typically served in Austria on New Year's Eve. To me, that reveals there is something special about it, and it makes sense—this salad even looks festive.

This can be served in a number of ways: Pair it with another of my most favorite tastes, Sardellenpaste (page 29) or a Liptauer (page 25), as an appetizer. Or, plate it individually on a bed of lettuce, as a first course. I like to save it as a starter, with wonderful black bread, or if I'm having a light summer meal with a selection of other salads.

Jarred herring is typically found in the refrigerated section of the supermarket, sometimes in the natural foods selection.

In a bowl, gently stir together all of the ingredients until combined. Cover with plastic wrap and chill.

When ready to serve, transfer the salad to a bowl. Store leftover salad in an airtight container in the refrigerator, for no more than 2 days.

CHOPPED LIVER

MAKES ABOUT 2 CUPS

We always had chopped liver for the high holy days and Passover. Oma made it the traditional way—with rendered chicken fat—as I suspect most everyone did at the time. She also chopped it by hand. (For a menu very like the one Oma served on Passover, see page 236.)

When I started to make chopped liver, I used chicken fat for a while, too, but then switched to olive oil for obvious reasons. And I gave in to the ease of using a food processor. My version is smoother than Oma's was; if you prefer more texture, chop it by hand.

❖

In a large skillet, heat the oil over medium-low heat until hot. Add the onion, and cook, stirring, until translucent and softened, 6 to 10 minutes. Do not let brown.

Add the chicken livers and salt to taste, and cook, stirring until the livers are browned on all sides and are no longer pink inside, about 15 minutes total. Remove the pan from the heat and let cool.

Transfer the contents of the skillet to a food processor fitted with the metal blade. Add the eggs, and process, chopping the eggs with the livers until the eggs are fully incorporated.

Scrape the chopped liver into a serving bowl, cover with plastic wrap, and chill. Serve with the chopped onion and challah, matzos, or crackers.

3 tablespoons extra-virgin olive oil
1 large onion, sliced
1 pound chicken livers, rinsed
Coarse kosher salt, to taste
3 extra-large eggs, hard-boiled (see page 32) and coarsely chopped
Chopped onion, for serving
Challah (page 58), matzos, or crackers, for serving

Note: If chicken livers are unavailable, which they were for me on one occasion, substitute 1 pound calves' liver. The result is superb.

Gefilte Fish

MAKES 16 PIECES

Making gefilte fish at home was something an earlier generation of cooks—our grandmothers and great-grandmothers—did. There are stories about how they did it, too, like the one whose grandmother kept the carp in the family bathtub. With store-bought gefilte fish, those wonderful anecdotes are passing.

This is actually my mother's recipe for gefilte fish. My friend Louise remembers it to this day, and describes it as "a taste you can't forget." Another friend, who remembers his own grandmother's homemade gefilte fish at their Passover seders, described it as the best he has ever tasted. The preparation cannot be done quickly. That said, I encourage you to try making it, and see if you agree.

❖

Have the fishmonger grind the whitefish and pike together for you along with the onion and carrot two times. (You can also do this in a food processor fitted with the metal blade.) Reserve the mixture, covered, in the refrigerator.

Make the fish broth: Put the reserved fish bones and heads in a large stockpot. Cover with 3 to 4 quarts water. Add the remaining broth ingredients and bring the liquid to a boil over medium-high heat. Reduce the heat to low and simmer, uncovered, for 45 minutes to 1 hour. Let stand until

---

A total of 5 pounds skinless fish fillets: 2½ pounds whitefish and 2½ pounds yellow pike, bones and fish heads reserved

1 onion

1 large carrot, peeled

FISH BROTH

The reserved bones and heads of the whitefish and yellow pike

4 small onions, sliced

5 medium carrots, peeled and left whole

¼ cup sugar

1 teaspoon coarse kosher salt

¼ teaspoon fresh pepper

FISH PIECES

3 extra-large eggs, separated

2 heaping tablespoons matzo cake meal

1 tablespoon sugar

2 teaspoons coarse kosher salt

¼ teaspoon fresh pepper

Apple-Horseradish Sauce (page 218), for serving

cool enough to handle, strain the broth into a large bowl, and then pour the strained broth back into the stockpot. Reserve the cooked carrots until serving time, refrigerating them in an airtight container if necessary.

Bring the strained broth to a simmer over medium-high heat.

While the broth comes to the boil, make the fish pieces: In a large bowl, combine the ground fish mixture with the 3 egg yolks, matzo meal, sugar, salt, and pepper. In a medium bowl with an electric mixer, beat the egg whites until they hold stiff peaks. Gently but thoroughly fold the beaten whites into the fish mixture until incorporated.

Using 2 large spoons or with dampened hands, form the mixture into 16 ovals, each about 2 inches long. Add the ovals to the broth, cover the pot, and simmer gently for 1½ hours. With a slotted spoon, remove the ovals to a large platter and let cool to room temperature. When cool, cover with plastic wrap and chill overnight. Transfer the broth to a clean container, let cool, and chill until it gels, best overnight.

To serve arrange the fish pieces on a large platter. Slice the reserved cooked carrots and arrange decoratively on the fish ovals. Serve with the horseradish sauce and a bowl of the jellied fish broth to pass at the table as an accompaniment.

LIPTAUER (FOUR WAYS)

At one of the first tasting gatherings for this book, I brought to the table two bowls of a mildly seasoned, savory spread of white cheese that throughout my childhood we always called Liptauer. At Oma's table, Liptauer was served with bread, challah, or even better, black bread. Typically it started the meal, and to me, it was always special, and very delicious.

At the tasting that evening we had a spirited crowd—as was always the case at our tastings. Among the tasters that night were my cousin Ruth Clapper, born in Vienna, a New Yorker for years now, and a skilled cook; Rita Grunwald, a dear friend, also born in Vienna who lives in Indianapolis with her Hungarian husband, John; Lisa Walborsky, Rita's godchild, another close friend, of Hungarian roots; and Elisabeth Pozzi-Thanner, a new and wonderful friend, also Austrian by birth, an oral historian, who happens to know a vast amount about Austrian food and cooking as well. Little did I know what I was about to unleash when I identified the bowls as two slightly different versions of Liptauer.

Liptauer, it turned out, was no idle conversation piece. It was close to the heart of everyone there. Some made it themselves, and if they didn't, they nonetheless had strong opinions about its ingredients, how it should be made, what it should look like, and how it should taste.

What was most amazing about the conversation that ensued, though, was that no two descriptions of their Liptauer were the same!

It was Austrian. No, it was Hungarian.

It was mild. No, it was spicy.

It was reddish. No, it was a deep red.

It should be smooth. No! It should have texture.

"There are caraway seeds—where are the caraway seeds?" someone asked. "They're meant to be cumin seeds, I think," said another. "There are no seeds in Liptauer," said someone else, putting an end to that line of thinking.

And last but most important, the anchovies. What about the anchovies? And how many?

I was sure that I remembered the flavor from all the times we had it when I was growing up. It was something my family loved, too. I thought Liptauer was made with cheese and some, though not too many, flavorings. But, now, *that* wasn't Liptauer?

And that was just the start. . . .

Liptauer (Fancy)

MAKES ABOUT 1 ½ CUPS

½ pound (8 ounces) ricotta
   cheese
8 tablespoons (1 stick) unsalted
   butter, softened
1 tablespoon sweet Hungarian
   paprika
¼ teaspoon coarse kosher salt
2 teaspoons caraway seeds
1 teaspoon dry mustard
1 teaspoon chopped drained
   capers
5 tablespoons chopped onion
Finely chopped chives, for
   rolling

Accompaniments: black bread,
   unsalted butter, finely
   chopped chives, sliced
   radishes, and chopped
   scallions

This version of Liptauer has caraway seeds, and a base of ricotta cheese and butter. (The one I remember—and loved—had anchovies. And there are no anchovies at all in this version; refer to the recipe that follows for the anchovy version.) The consensus of our tasters: The amount of chopped onion in this version was tasty, but more paprika was needed (which I have since added to the recipe). By all counts, the accompaniments were delicious. And so was the way it was served, rolled in fresh chives. This version of Liptauer may not have been exactly as any of our Liptauer-loving group remembered it, but we certainly ate our fair share.

❖

In a food processor fitted with the metal blade, process the ricotta, butter, paprika, salt, caraway seeds, mustard, capers, and onion until smooth. Scrape into a bowl, cover with plastic wrap, and chill, 45 minutes to 1 hour.

To serve, shape the Liptauer into a mound and roll in the chopped chives. Serve on a platter with suggested accompaniments.

Liptauer with Anchovies

MAKES ABOUT 2½ CUPS

I n my personal view, this version of Liptauer is closest to what I remember enjoying as a young girl, though somehow it's still not quite the same. My cousin Ruth said it was all about the texture; it needed more texture. I wasn't sure.

At least we'd located the anchovies, a wonderful find. As to the number of anchovies, that was another question. The consensus on this try: good, but still not *the one*. (For those who want more anchovies, see the following recipe.) Experiment for yourself to discover what you like—and remember—best.

❖

1 pound (16 ounces) cream cheese, at room temperature

8 tablespoons (1 stick) unsalted butter, softened

¼ cup sour cream

5 anchovy fillets, drained and chopped

¼ cup drained capers

4 teaspoons sweet Hungarian paprika

Black bread, for serving

Chopped chives, for garnish

In a food processor fitted with the metal blade, process all the ingredients until smooth. Scrape the spread into a serving bowl, cover with plastic wrap, and chill 45 minutes to 1 hour.

Shortly before serving, remove and let stand at room temperature to soften.

To serve, spread the Liptauer on black bread, then sprinkle chives on top.

Liptauer with (More) Anchovies

MAKES ABOUT 2 TO 2¼ CUPS

12 ounces whole-milk cottage cheese

½ pound (8 ounces) cream cheese, at room temperature

8 tablespoons (1 stick) unsalted butter, softened

8 anchovy fillets, drained and chopped

1 teaspoon capers, drained

2 tablespoons sweet Hungarian paprika

Black bread, for serving

In our grand Liptauer journey we moved from ricotta and butter (Fancy) to cream cheese, butter, sour cream, and anchovies to this version, which uses cottage cheese, cream cheese, butter, sour cream, and *more anchovies*.

We were getting closer, but . . .

In a food processor fitted with the metal blade, process all of the ingredients until smooth. Scrape the mixture into a serving bowl, cover with plastic wrap, and chill 45 minutes to 1 hour.

Shortly before serving time, remove the bowl from the refrigerator and let stand at room temperature to soften and become spreadable. Serve with the black bread.

Store leftover Liptauer, covered, in the refrigerator. And then I made this:

My Most Favorite "Liptauer" (Thanks to Oma)

Combine all ingredients in a bowl and mash together *by hand.*

"This is the one!" went up the roar. This is the one that I (and everyone else that day) absolutely loved.

P.S.: You may be wondering why I have put Liptauer in quotation marks. Here is why. When I served it, calling it yet another version of Liptauer, Elisabeth Pozzi-Thanner, who makes her own Liptauer (with sweet paprika; chopped onion; a little yogurt; ricotta that is creamy, not too curd-y; chopped chives and parsley; cumin seeds; salt; and a hint of honey mustard!—another version entirely) replied, "Ah, '*Sardellenpaste.*' Anchovy spread!"

And so it goes. We had arrived at a Liptauer, and, discovered something intriguing along the way: Depending on where you are from, Liptauer is the way you remember it. Each of us has a unique memory of it, recalled with different ingredients and a range of colors and flavors, *and* great passion.

4 ounces cream cheese, softened

8 tablespoons (1 stick) unsalted butter, softened

1 2-ounce can anchovy fillets, drained and chopped

1½ tablespoons sweet Hungarian paprika

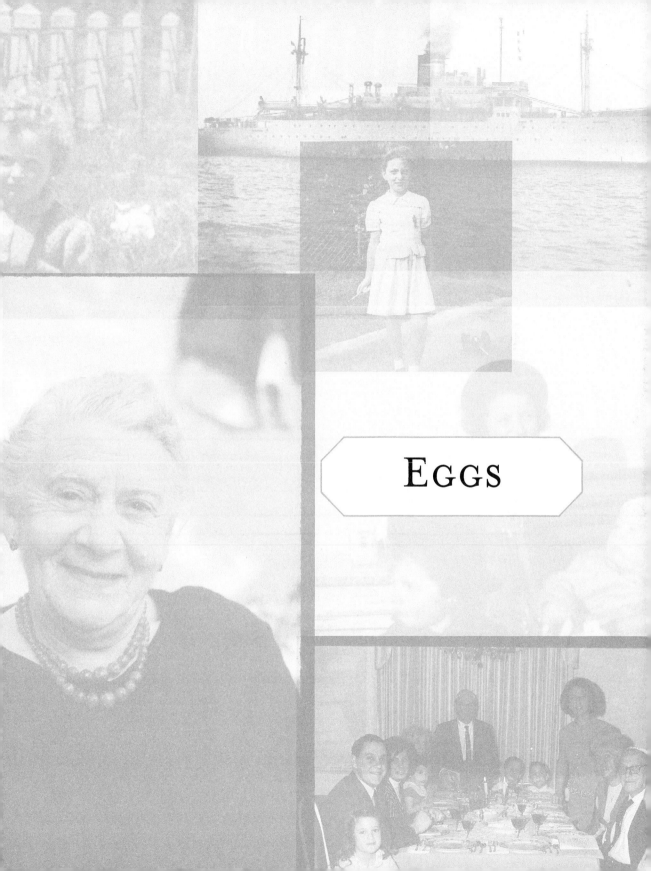

EGGS

DEVILED EGGS

MAKES 18 HALVES

9 extra-large eggs

2 tablespoons mayonnaise,
or more, if desired

1 teaspoon dry mustard

Coarse kosher salt and fresh
pepper, to taste

Sweet Hungarian paprika, for
garnish

There was a time when deviled eggs fell out of fashion—for health reasons, no doubt—but in my household, they never lost their popularity. Whenever I make these, people love them.

I have served these with Liptauer (page 29) and was surprised to learn from Elisabeth that plain hard-boiled eggs are a typical accompaniment for the spread in her home country of Austria. Some combinations just seem to find each other naturally.

To hard-boil eggs: Lay the eggs gently in a large saucepan and cover with cold water. Bring the water to a boil over medium-high heat. Reduce the heat to a gentle simmer and boil for 10 minutes, no longer. Remove the pan from the heat, and with a slotted spoon transfer the eggs to a large bowl of ice water. Let cool.

When cool, peel the eggs, halve them, remove the yolks, and place them in a bowl. Mash the yolks with a fork, add mayonnaise and mustard, and combine well. Season with salt and pepper to taste.

Mound the filling into each of the cooked whites and arrange the filled halves on a platter. Before serving, dust lightly with paprika.

A Brief Note on the Jewish Dietary Laws

The Jewish dietary laws, or *Kashrut,* are spelled out in the Torah in certain verses of the books of Exodus, Deuteronomy, and Leviticus. These laws prohibit the consumption of certain foods, specifically certain meats and certain fish, and the combination of certain foods. Permissible foods include:

- the meat of animals that chew the cud and have cloven hooves (all pork products are, by definition, excluded)
- fish that have both fins and scales (any shellfish or bottomfish are thus excluded).

In addition, any dishes with meat and milk (or their derivatives) cannot be eaten together in the same meal. Neither can meat and milk dishes be cooked together at the same time. Separate cooking equipment, including pots, utensils, and/or plates, is required for the preparation of meat dishes and dairy dishes. Storage of such foods must also be separate.

The word *pareve*, sometimes also spelled *parve*, defines a foodstuff that is neutral, meaning it contains no meat or milk (or a derivative of either) and is thus suitable to be eaten with both meat and dairy. Examples of pareve ingredients include vegetables, pasta, and rice, to name just a few. The symbol of a circled Ⓤ or a circled Ⓚ on the packaging or the label of an ingredient indicates that the product has been certified as kosher pareve.

"Keeping kosher" means to observe the Jewish dietary laws. How one observes the Jewish dietary laws, and to what extent, is a highly personal matter.

This brief explanation of the Jewish dietary laws clarifies why I have included several *all*-dairy menus (see pages 240 and 241) at the end of the book. In the Desserts chapter, I have also noted in several recipe headnotes that margarine can be substituted for butter in order for the recipe to comply with a menu that includes meat.

EGGS WITH
SAUTÉED ONIONS

SERVES 6 AS A SPREAD

6 extra-large eggs, hard-boiled,
    cooled, and peeled (see
    page 32)
2 tablespoons flavorless
    vegetable oil
1 cup chopped onion (1 medium-
    large)
Coarse kosher salt and fresh
    pepper, to taste
Crackers, matzos, or bread,
    for serving

I call this a spread, but it makes a good sandwich filling, too, especially with rye bread. With no special ingredients needed, and a simple preparation, it also is a nice complement to a first-course green salad.

❖

Put the eggs in a bowl and coarsely chop.

Heat the oil in a medium skillet over medium heat until hot. Add the onion, and cook, stirring, until translucent and softened, about 4 minutes.

Stir in the chopped eggs, and cook just to combine with the onion. Taste, season with salt and pepper, and transfer to a serving bowl. Serve with crackers.

My Mother's Omelet with French Fries

MAKES 1 OMELET

Instead of serving French fries as an accompaniment to this omelet, my mother was inspired to add the fried potatoes right into the eggs. The result? A plate of the best kind of comfort food.

Make this for brunch, lunch, or a light supper with a green salad and black bread to round out the meal.

❖

1 medium-to-large Idaho potato

Flavorless vegetable oil, for deep-frying

2 extra-large eggs

Coarse kosher salt and fresh pepper, to taste

1 tablespoon unsalted butter

½ to 1 tablespoon chopped fresh parsley

Bring a medium saucepan of water to a boil over high heat. Meanwhile, peel the potato and cut it into strips, about ¼ inch wide. When the water comes to a boil, add the potato strips, and blanch for 5 minutes. Drain in a colander. Transfer the potato to paper towels and let cool in a single layer for 5 minutes.

While the potato strips cool, heat about ½ inch of the oil in a wide heavy saucepan until hot, 350 degrees F on a deep-fat thermometer. Add the potato strips and deep-fry until golden brown, about 5 minutes (or longer if you like them crispier), turning them as needed. Remove the potatoes with a slotted spoon to paper towels to drain.

In a bowl, beat the eggs until combined, season with salt and pepper to taste, and stir in the potatoes, covering them with the beaten eggs.

In an 8-inch nonstick skillet, melt the butter over medium-high heat. When the foam subsides, add the egg mixture. Cook until the eggs are set on the bottom, about 3 minutes. If desired, sprinkle in ½ tablespoon of the parsley. Flip the omelet and cook until the second side is set, 2 to 3 minutes. Sprinkle with the remaining ½ tablespoon parsley, slip the omelet onto a plate, and serve.

VEGETABLE FRITTATA

MAKES 8 SERVINGS AS A FIRST COURSE

You may wonder how a frittata came to be in a cookbook by someone who was raised in an Austrian-Jewish household in Queens, New York. Spending the first five years of my life in Italy, before we came to the United States as refugees, has forever made Italy a special place for me. I love Italy and go there often. It was, and still is, a haven for me—its food, its people, and many warm memories.

This frittata is filled with a variety of fresh vegetables and wonderful flavor. Frittata, remember, can be served shortly after being removed from the oven, or it can be cooled to warm. Serve it for brunch, with salad, or for a light, late dinner, with good bread.

Preheat the oven to 350 degrees F. Grease a 10-inch-round, 2-inch-deep cake pan, and set aside.

In a large skillet, heat the oil over medium-high heat until hot but not smoking. Add the onion, garlic, squash, bell peppers, and mushrooms and sauté, stirring, until cooked, but still crisp-tender, about 20 minutes. Remove from the heat to cool slightly.

In a large bowl, whisk together the eggs, cream, salt, and pepper. Stir in the croutons until combined, then add the cream cheese and Swiss cheese and stir well again. Stir in the sautéed vegetables until completely incorporated.

3 tablespoons olive oil

1 large Spanish onion, thinly sliced

3 garlic cloves, minced

3 summer squash, ends removed and sliced ¼ inch thick

3 zucchini, ends removed and sliced ¼ inch thick

3 bell peppers (a red, a green, and a yellow) cored, seeded, and ribs removed, and cut into ½-inch strips

½ pound (8 ounces) sliced mushrooms

6 extra-large eggs

¼ cup heavy cream

1 teaspoon coarse kosher salt

1 teaspoon fresh pepper

2 cups stale plain croutons, from day-old French bread

½ pound (8 ounces) cream cheese, cut into small cubes

2 cups grated Swiss cheese

Pour the mixture into the prepared pan and level the top. Bake about 1 hour, until firm. Check at the halfway point, and if the top is browning too quickly, lay a piece of foil loosely over the top of the pan.

Let stand 10 to 15 minutes to rest before serving slightly warm, when the fritatta is at its very best.

SOUPS

CHICKEN SOUP

MAKES ABOUT 4½ QUARTS

1 whole kosher chicken
(4 pounds), giblets included
and livers removed and
discarded, rinsed

Coarse kosher salt, to taste

3 large carrots, peeled

3 large stalks celery, trimmed

1 large sweet potato, peeled

1 large parsnip, peeled

1 large turnip, peeled

1 large onion, unpeeled

8 whole garlic cloves, peeled

1 handful fresh parsley sprigs

1 handful fresh dill sprigs

1 teaspoon black peppercorns

Matzo Balls (page 43), Farina
Dumplings (page 156), or soup
noodles

On Fridays, after Oma had come back from grocery shopping, she would start this soup. She always added the onion unpeeled, which I do, too—a direct carryover from her. The peel adds color to the soup base, and it's a nice old-fashioned touch. The addition of dill is mine. Dill was not in Oma's vernacular.

Oma typically added Goodman's noodles to her soup. I make mine with matzo balls, which tells you a little something about how recipes evolve when they are handed down. In her later years, when I first had my own household, Oma would come stay with me, and we would cook together, giving and taking what we liked best about each other's way of doing things. That said, what I would not alter about Oma's Friday night dinner is the Brisket (page 69) that always followed this soup.

It is amazing how often you can make something, and then learn an essential about it. That happened with this recipe when I was testing it for this book. The amount of salt you add is very important. Too little and you will hear it from your dinner guests. Too much, and you'll hear about that, too. Taste and adjust the salt judiciously before you serve this soup.

❖

Into a stockpot or a large soup pot, pour 5 quarts (20 cups) water. Add the chicken and giblets plus 2 tablespoons kosher salt and bring the water to a boil over medium-high heat. As the water heats, scum will rise to the surface. Skim as much of it as possible off with a large spoon. When most of the foam has been removed and the water is beginning to boil, add all the vegetables along with the garlic, parsley sprigs, dill sprigs, and peppercorns. Cook, uncovered, at a high simmer for 45 minutes, skimming off the foam when necessary.

After 45 minutes, reduce the heat to medium-low, cover the pot, and cook for 1¼ to 1½ hours.

Carefully remove the hot chicken from the pot to a platter. (If it falls apart, either serve it as is in pieces, or arrange it the best you can on the platter.) Cover to keep warm. Leave the vegetables in the soup pot, covered, until serving time.

Add the matzo balls to the pot and allow them to heat in the soup, if needed. Taste the soup for seasonings, and add salt to taste. Ladle soup and a matzo ball into each soup plate and add carrots or other of the cooked soup vegetables, as desired. Remove the remaining vegetables to the platter of boiled chicken, and serve either whole or slice them on the platter.

Depending upon how many people you are serving, you may have quite a bit of leftover soup. My advice is to let it cool, then divide it into smaller containers (quart-sized is convenient), and freeze the soup for up to 2 months.

Matzo Balls and More

My grandmother did all the shopping for our meals on foot, and she shopped almost every day. She had a route: the A&P on 164th Street and Union Turnpike for fruit and vegetables, then onto the kosher butcher on 167th Street and Union Turnpike, then back home to 167th and 82nd Avenue. It had to be at least a mile each way, and I can remember being amazed that she could do this day after day. If she ever forgot anything, I'd have to run to the store. It was then that I realized what a fast walker she was.

There was one outing that was different, though: going to Streit's on Rivington Street on the Lower East Side. When it came to matzo, my grandmother would only buy it from Streit's—and that meant taking the car.

We would all pile into my uncle's car and wait while Oma bought matzos, matzo meal, soup nuts, fruit slices, and whatever else she needed.

I am happy to say that as of this writing, Streit's is still there.

Here are a few ways that Oma used matzo—recipes I treasure and still prepare today.

MATZO BALLS

MAKES 8 LARGE MATZO BALLS

Oma's matzo balls were not fluffy. They were somewhat soft on the outside, harder in the center. I used cake meal in this recipe to come closer to what I remember Oma's matzo balls to be like. It worked.

If you prefer matzo balls that are soft throughout, use only ¾ cup cake meal. Of course, matzo balls are typically made with matzo meal. If using matzo meal, simply follow the directions on the box.

In a bowl, whisk together the eggs, oil, seltzer, 1 teaspoon salt, and pepper to taste. Whisk in the cake meal until fully blended. Stir in the fresh herbs, if using. Cover the bowl with plastic wrap and refrigerate for 30 minutes.

While the mix is chilling, bring a large soup pot of water with 3 tablespoons salt to a boil over high heat.

Make matzo balls by shaping enough of the mixture to fill the palm of your hand into round balls. Add to the boiling water, reduce the heat to a simmer, and cook, uncovered, for 30 to 35 minutes. The matzo balls will fluff in size and rise to the surface. With a slotted spoon, transfer them to a colander. Add them to your soup, or let cool, then transfer to a freezer bag. Freeze individually, or two to a bag, or in larger quantities for up to 3 months. To serve, add the frozen matzo balls to your soup pot and

4 extra-large eggs

¼ cup flavorless vegetable oil

¼ cup seltzer

1 teaspoon plus 3 tablespoons coarse kosher salt

Pinch fresh pepper

1 cup matzo cake meal

¾ tablespoon chopped fresh dill (optional)

¾ tablespoon chopped fresh parsley (optional)

heat over gentle heat for about 30 minutes, or until thawed. (The heating time will depend upon how many matzo balls you add to the soup.)

MATZO BREI

MAKES 3 TO 4 SERVINGS

My husband, Marvin, perfected this recipe. During Passover, when our kids were young, they would wait with bated breath around the stove for breakfast: "Is it ready yet?" was the chorus. I felt that way too. I still love this comforting egg and matzo combination. It is filling and delicious, and though we had it in the morning, you can also make extra and nosh on it from the pan over the course of the day. Something I also love to do.

1¼ cups whole milk

5 sheets matzo, broken into medium pieces

5 extra-large eggs

½ teaspoon coarse kosher salt

Pinch fresh pepper

1½ tablespoons unsalted butter, or more, as needed

1½ tablespoons flavorless vegetable oil, or more, as needed

In a large pot, stir together the milk and broken matzo until combined. Place the pan over medium heat and cook, stirring, 4 to 5 minutes, until the matzo is softened.

Break the eggs into a bowl, and add the salt and pepper to taste. Stir until combined. Stir in the warm matzo mixture.

In a 12-inch skillet, melt the butter with the oil over medium heat. Add the matzo-egg mixture, pat it into the pan, and cook until lightly browned on the bottom, 5 to 6 minutes. Turn the mixture over (if it breaks don't worry) and cook until lightly browned on the second side. Serve at once because if your family is anything like mine, they will be waiting for it.

Note: I like savory matzo brei. Other people love to dip the pieces in maple syrup.

MATZO COFFEE

8 ounces fresh-brewed hot
    coffee
Milk to taste
Sugar to taste
Matzo

During Passover, my father would add matzo to his coffee because he loved the taste of softened coffee-flavored matzo. Matzo Coffee, as it came to be called, became a family tradition. To this day, I cannot wait for the morning of the first day of Passover.

Here is how I make each cup:

Add milk and sweeten the coffee as desired. Sugar is a must. Then break off one-quarter of the sheet of matzo, break it into pieces, and stir it into the coffee. Enjoy your matzo coffee with a spoon. Keep adding one-quarter more of the matzo, broken up, to your coffee when needed, as you also replenish the coffee, milk, and sugar.

BEEF BROTH

MAKES 5 QUARTS

I like to make a lot of beef broth. It freezes well and you never know when you might want a bowl, with matzo balls or dumplings.

In addition to a lot of soup, you reap another dividend when you prepare this recipe: the main course—flanken with vegetables. Traditional food in some households, it is comforting and filling, and requires no special cooking skills, just a big pot and enough time for the meat to simmer—at least 2½ hours. Your house will smell wonderful, and you will have food for days.

Put the broth on to cook, then make the dumplings. If you prefer, substitute Matzo Balls (page 43). Be sure to skim the broth as it cooks.

❖

In a stockpot or large soup pot, combine the flanken, water, and salt, and bring to a boil over medium-high heat. As the water heats, scum will rise to the surface; remove as much of it as possible with a large spoon.

When the meat has cooked about 15 minutes, add all the remaining ingredients, except the dumplings. Simmer for 2 to 2½ hours, skimming the scum from the surface when necessary.

With a slotted spoon, remove the flanken, carrots, turnips, and parsnips to a large platter and tent with foil to keep warm if serving as a main course following the soup.

3 pounds beef flanken

Scant 6 quarts water

1½ tablespoons coarse kosher salt

2 large carrots, peeled

3 whole leeks, trimmed and well rinsed

4 stalks celery

3 plum tomatoes

3 turnips, trimmed and peeled

3 parsnips, peeled

1 large onion

12 garlic cloves, peeled

1 small handful black peppercorns

1 small handful fresh parsley sprigs

1 small handful fresh dill sprigs

Farina Dumplings (page 156)

(For how to serve, see page 68.) If serving at another time, let cool, cover tightly with foil, and refrigerate.

Strain the broth into a large clean pot. Pick out the cooked garlic cloves and reserve. Discard the vegetables, herbs, and peppercorns in the sieve. Mash the softened garlic cloves through the sieve into the strained broth and stir.

Add the farina dumplings to the broth and taste the soup for seasonings. Gently reheat the soup over medium-low heat until the dumplings are heated through. Serve in wide soup bowls.

Store leftover broth in airtight containers in the refrigerator for 3 days, or freeze for up to 2 months.

BORSCHT

I cannot remember exactly how Oma celebrated the holiday of Shavuous, when only dairy is allowed, but she may have served a borscht of some kind. This rendition is mine, much richer than anything Oma might have made, and is almost ruby-like in color. Since it is made in advance this soup is perfect for summer entertaining. Serve it in small white cups, demitasse size, if you have them.

Use Vegetable Broth (page 51), if you like, in place of the water for additional flavor.

❖

In a large pot, bring the water with the whole onion, sugar, lemon juice, and salt to a boil over medium-high heat. Add the chopped beets and simmer, uncovered, until tender when pierced with a fork, about 45 minutes. Let the mixture cool.

Fit a food processor with the metal blade. Put the cucumber and halved onion in the workbowl and process until chopped. Start adding the cooled beet mixture through the feed tube, and puree. (If necessary, transfer the first batch of puree to a large plastic container.) Finish pureeing the remaining beet mixture. Add the sour cream to the workbowl and process until incorporated. Add the chopped dill and process again. Pour all the soup into a

10 cups water

1 small onion, peeled but left whole

1 teaspoon sugar

1 teaspoon fresh lemon juice

¾ tablespoon coarse kosher salt

2 pounds beets, trimmed of greens, washed, peeled, and coarsely chopped

½ large cucumber, peeled and coarsely chopped

½ onion, chopped

2 cups (1 pint) sour cream, plus additional, for serving

1 handful chopped fresh dill

Chopped chives, for garnish

Fresh pepper, to taste

large container, stir to combine, and cover. Refrigerate until well chilled, several hours at least.

When ready to serve, season the borscht with salt and pepper to taste. Ladle the soup into cups or small soup bowls and garnish each serving with a dollop of sour cream and a sprinkling of chopped chives.

VEGETABLE BROTH

MAKES 6 TO 7 CUPS

I make my own vegetable broth. Oma relied on Washington's, a brand consistent with the dietary laws, which requires nothing more than dissolving packets of powder in boiling water. If you have an hour, make mine; if you don't, do what Oma did. Washington's is still on the market today.

In a medium soup pot, combine the water with all the vegetables, garlic, and herb sprigs. Season with salt to taste and a spoonful of peppercorns and bring the mixture to a boil over high heat. Reduce the heat to low, and simmer gently, uncovered, for 1 hour.

Strain the broth into a clean pot and adjust the seasonings. The cooled broth can be stored in a covered container in the refrigerator for 3 days, or frozen for 2 weeks.

8 cups water
2 carrots, peeled
4 stalks celery
2 small tomatoes, quartered
6 garlic cloves, peeled
Several sprigs *each* fresh
     parsley, thyme, and dill
Coarse kosher salt and whole
     peppercorns, to taste

Sweet-and-Sour Tomato-Cabbage Soup

MAKES 6 TO 8 SERVINGS

4 cups tomato juice

4 cups water

6 cups Beef Broth (page 47), Vegetable Broth (page 51), or pareve soup base powder dissolved in water (see Note below)

5 cups finely shredded cored green cabbage (about 1 pound)

3 cups coarsely chopped onions (about 4)

2 teaspoons minced garlic

3 tablespoons granulated sugar

1 tablespoon brown sugar

2 teaspoons fresh lemon juice

Oma liked cabbage, especially in vegetable side dishes (see Krautfleckerl, page 135). I like it in a variety of ways, including stuffed (page 74) and also in soup—especially this one, which is notably sweet, with strips of silky, soft cabbage, and an unforgettable color. All you need is one pot and an hour. You won't believe the results.

❖

In a large soup pot, combine all the ingredients. Bring to a boil over medium heat and cook, stirring occasionally, for 1 hour.

To serve, ladle into cups or small bowls, and serve hot.

Note: If you observe the dietary laws, use pareve meat-style powder. You will need 1 tablespoon powder per 2 cups water.

Vegetable Soup

My mother worked every day, as did her sister, my aunt Ciel, who also lived with us. Neither was a cook, they hadn't the time to be. Oma saw to our food and its preparation.

One notable exception, for me, was a day when I was home sick while still in grade school. My mother made this soup for me. That was such a special occurrence and I enjoyed it so much, that I have never forgotten it.

My mother never passed down the recipe. If this is not an exact replica, it is very close to it, and I love it to this day. The addition of margarine at the end, for body, is mine.

My Austrian friend Elisabeth tells me that there is a winter version of vegetable soup, as well—made with winter vegetables. (I'd say this one is early fall.) In other words, feel free to use vegetables that are available, ones you like, whatever the time of year.

❖

In a large soup pot, combine all the ingredients except the margarine, and bring to a boil over medium-high heat. Cover the pot, reduce the heat to low, and simmer for 1½ to 2 hours, stirring occasionally. (The longer the soup cooks, the thicker it will get.)

During the last 30 minutes of cooking, add the margarine, stirring occasionally until melted and incorporated.

Serve the soup in wide bowls, with bread of your choice,

1 pound dried navy beans, soaked overnight in cold water to cover, and drained

4 cups chopped onions (5 large)

4 garlic cloves, minced

3 cups chopped peeled tomatoes (3 large)

12 cups (a double recipe) Vegetable Broth (page 51), store-bought ready-to-use broth, or Washington's Seasoning and Broth packets made according to the directions

6 cups water

1½ bay leaves, crumbled

2 fresh thyme sprigs

1 cup chopped fresh parsley

4 stalks celery, chopped

4 carrots, peeled and sliced medium-thick

3 medium zucchini, ends trimmed and sliced

Coarse kosher salt and fresh pepper, to taste

8 tablespoons (1 stick) unsalted margarine, cut into pieces

as a first course, or as a meal in itself. The soup keeps in a covered container in the refrigerator for 5 days and can be frozen for 2 months. Depending upon how long you cooked the soup, you may need to add water to thin it when you reheat it.

WOMEN OF A KIND

My mother, like her own mother, had been a businesswoman when she and my father were living in Vienna before the outbreak of war. And then the war came, and nothing was the same for either my grandmother or my mother—not homeland, not family, not language, not anything. The turn their lives took required them to be resilient and strong, or maybe the word is *stronger*. But that was only part of it. Once on American shores, they had to build new lives for themselves and their families.

I was able to observe the singular qualities of these women when we were all living under the same roof in Queens. Oma was head of the household; my mother went to work every day. Being only nine or ten years old at the time, I wasn't yet able to identify the character traits these two brave women embodied. All I knew was that I admired them and the way they went about doing things. Presence and fortitude are words I would use now to describe them.

Years passed. I grew up, married, and had five of the most marvelous children. We lived in the suburbs with a dog and station wagon. But somewhere, in the back of my psyche, were the images of the two strong women I had watched as a young girl. I wanted to be like them.

In 1982 I went into business with my dear friend Marsha Ozer. Together we leased a small retail space in Great Neck, Long Island, where we baked cakes, then sold them to restaurants and outlets in New York City. The name of the company was My Most Favorite Dessert Company. One day over dinner Marsha told me that she had had enough of the baking business. I can't say that her news surprised me. What was incredible, though, was that we were able to part ways and still maintain a wonderful friendship, which exists to this day.

And so it began. My Most Favorite Dessert Company moved into Manhattan in 1986 to a space near Eighty-Sixth Street on Madison Avenue. At that time we were still selling fine pastries and baked goods, but the rent on Madison Avenue was not cheap even then, so I decided to serve lunch. It would be simple fare, but it would be served nonetheless. What to serve? Without even having to think about it, my mother's soups came to mind. In addition to her unforgettable Vegetable Soup (page 53), she had also made one with split peas. My mother's recipe for split pea soup was the first offering on our newly expanded menu. The customers took to our lunches of soups, salads, and sandwiches.

We were open for both breakfast and lunch, but as so often it happens the rent bills kept right on coming. I decided to serve dinner. And here is where I realized just how formative those early years of living in Italy had been for me. Italian cuisine was what I would offer on the dinner menu—pastas, fresh salads, homemade bread. I would use only seasonal ingredients, freshly prepared, as you would have them in Italy.

Note the influences: Viennese-style baked goods, with a few favorite American offerings such as muffins and carrot loaf, for breakfast; to an American-style informal lunch menu of soup, salads, and sandwiches; to a dinner menu of Italian favorites. It was all interconnected: I was serving dishes that reflected the happiest times in my life.

The inspiration for it all? Oma and my mother.

My mother, Berta, and two of her great-grandchildren, Reuben and Lila Chess, visiting

Fort Ontario, which had been our family's first home in America.

BREADS

CHALLAH

MAKES 4 LOAVES, EACH ABOUT 9 INCHES IN DIAMETER

2 tablespoons dry yeast or
   3 envelopes Fleischmann's
   Traditional Yeast
¾ cup warm (11 degrees) water
2 teaspoons plus ½ cup sugar
8 tablespoons (1 stick) unsalted
   margarine
1 cup boiling water
¼ cup honey
¼ cup flavorless vegetable oil
2 tablespoons coarse kosher
   salt
8 extra-large eggs
10 cups all-purpose flour
1 cup raisins (optional)
1 egg yolk plus 1 teaspoon water,
   for egg wash

During the week, we had rye bread and black bread. Challah was for Friday. These homemade loaves are perfectly beautiful looking—and out-of-this world good. If you like, make two plain loaves and two with raisins, for a little variety.

❖

Using a 1-quart measuring cup, dissolve the yeast in the warm water, add 2 teaspoons sugar, and set the cup aside in a warm place to proof the yeast, about 5 minutes, or until it is foamy, with bubbles on the top.

In the large bowl of a standing electric mixer, combine the margarine and boiling water and stir until the margarine is melted. Stir in the remaining ½ cup sugar, honey, oil, and salt until combined. Add the eggs, one at a time, beating well after each addition. Mix in the proofed yeast mixture and blend on medium speed until combined.

Reduce the mixer speed to low and gradually add 9 cups of the flour. Blend until a dough forms. Stir in the raisins, if using, mixing until they are evenly distributed. Turn the dough out on a well-floured surface and knead it gently, working in ½ cup of the remaining flour, until it feels very silky and is elastic to the touch. Shape the dough into a round, transfer it to a large, clean bowl, cover it with plastic wrap, and let it stand for 1 to 2 hours, until doubled in bulk.

Punch down the dough and knead it again to reshape it into a round. Divide the dough into 4 equal pieces.

Roll each piece into a long rope, about 22 inches long, on a floured surface. Holding one end with your left hand, twist the rope counterclockwise around itself until a round spiral is formed. Tuck the end under and pinch to seal to the dough. Repeat with the remaining 3 ropes of dough. Place 2 challahs on each of 2 large baking sheets, cover with plastic wrap, and let rise in a warm place until doubled in bulk, about 1 hour.

While the loaves are rising, preheat the oven to 350 degrees F. In a cup, stir together the egg yolk and water. Brush each of the loaves with the egg wash.

Bake the breads for 25 to 30 minutes, or until golden brown. Transfer the challahs to wire racks to cool.

Store each challah in a plastic bag at room temperature for up to 2 days. Or put the bread in a freezer bag and freeze up to 3 months.

CORN BREAD

MAKES 2 7½ × 4-INCH LOAVES

2 cups all-purpose flour

¾ cup yellow cornmeal

1 teaspoon baking powder

½ teaspoon coarse kosher salt

1½ cups soy milk

1 teaspoon baking soda

¾ cup sugar

½ cup flavorless vegetable oil

2 extra-large eggs

1 teaspoon pure vanilla extract

My daughter Renée and I occasionally give cooking classes, and one fall we taught one on Thanksgiving side dishes: corn bread, corn bread stuffing, cranberry chutney, and so on. With Renée's permission, I'm sharing this simple, very good recipe. If you should have any left over, toast it, then add a little jam for a wonderful snack.

Preheat the oven to 375 degrees F. Grease two 7½ × 4-inch loaf pans and set aside.

In a bowl, whisk together the flour, cornmeal, baking powder, and salt.

In another bowl, stir together the soy milk and baking soda until the baking soda is dissolved.

In a large bowl, beat the sugar and oil together until well combined. Beat in the eggs, one at a time, then stir in the vanilla. Add the flour mixture in three additions to the egg mixture, alternating with the soy milk mixture, beating just until blended.

Divide the batter between the prepared pans and bake for 35 to 40 minutes, or until a cake tester inserted in the center comes out clean. Let the loaves cool in the pans for 10 minutes before removing them to a wire rack to cool completely.

BREAD CRUMBS

Just as Oma had a set route for when she went shopping, she had a set number of dishes she made, and she didn't deviate from those. What she cooked was predictable and comforting, and those dishes—whole menus, even—became favorites of mine: her Friday-night dinner with her brisket, soups, apple cake, *and* her toasted bread crumbs. Whatever she added them to, whether it was noodles or vegetables, was transformed into something delicious. I learned years later that crumbs are used like that in traditional Austrian cooking. But they were not typical to me—they were special.

Because my grandmother observed the dietary laws, she used margarine. Butter makes them tasty, too. You can also toast plain store-bought bread crumbs, which I am sure Oma did when she ran out of time to make her own.

HOMEMADE
BREAD CRUMBS

Let the bread you have—it can be French, Italian, or sliced white or whole-wheat bread—become stale. Tear it into pieces and leave on the counter overnight, or toast in the oven until dry. Then grind it in a food processor fitted with the metal blade, to fine crumbs. Pour the crumbs into an airtight container and store them in the freezer.

Toasted Homemade Bread Crumbs

Melt the margarine in a large (depending upon the amount of crumbs you are toasting) nonstick skillet over low heat. Add the crumbs, directly from the freezer, and stir them into the margarine. They will clump at first. Stir constantly, otherwise they burn in a matter of seconds. The crumbs will start to separate and turn a lovely golden brown, and the most wonderful aroma of toast will rise from the skillet. Remove immediately from the heat. One cup of crumbs usually takes 4 to 5 minutes to toast; larger amounts will take as much as 10 minutes.

Note: In these pages you will find toasted crumbs with cauliflower, Savoy cabbage, and pasta. Don't stop there. Try them on Brussels sprouts, egg noodles, and on and on. They contribute much more than what you might suspect.

For every cup of crumbs, you will need 2 tablespoons (¼ stick) unsalted margarine or butter

Main Courses

Beef and Veal ♦ 67

Flanken with Vegetables ♦ Brisket ♦ Cholent ♦ Stuffed Cabbage ♦ *Fleischlabel* (Chopped Meat Patties) ♦ Meat Kabobs ♦ Meat Loaf ♦ Stuffed Peppers ♦ Beef Goulash with Carrots and Potatoes ♦ Shell Steak with Onions ♦ *Wiener Schnitzel* (Viennese Veal Cutlets) ♦ Veal Stew with Tomatoes and Green Pepper ♦ Veal Stew with Mushrooms ♦ Veal Roast with Roasted Fresh Vegetables ♦ Calves' Liver with Apples and Onions

Poultry ♦ 99

Orange-Glazed Chicken ♦ Roast Chicken with Bread Stuffing ♦ My Mother's Chicken Paprika ♦ My Chicken Cutlets ♦ *Backhendl* (Fried Chicken, Viennese Style) ♦ Apricot-Stuffed Chicken Breasts ♦ Lemon Chicken ♦ Pepper Ragout with Sausage ♦ Roast Turkey with Apple, Almond, and Raisin Stuffing ♦ Turkey Pot Pie

Fish ♦ 121

Fresh Salmon Cakes ♦ Fried Flounder ♦ Fried Halibut Fingers

BEEF AND VEAL

Flanken with Vegetables

Makes 8 Generous Servings

Flanken and vegetables (the carrots, turnips, and parsnips) removed from Beef Broth
Apple-Horseradish Sauce (page 218)

When you make Beef Broth (page 47), you automatically become the beneficiary of this wonderful old-fashioned dish: flanken with an assortment of soup vegetables. It is one-pot cooking at its very best, the kind many grandmothers always seem to excel in.

Place the flanken in the middle of a serving platter and surround with the vegetables. Serve with the horseradish sauce.

BRISKET

MAKES 8 GENEROUS SERVINGS

Oma's Friday night dinner was always brisket, preceded by her Chicken Soup (page 40). She would begin cooking early on Friday, after she shopped. When I came home from school, I would run downstairs to the kitchen to check on the pot of simmering meat. I don't think she ever knew that I cut off a little piece—just a taste! It was so delicious, and even though dinner was at six o'clock sharp every night, as it was every night, it was a long wait till the next even more delicious taste.

For two Friday night dinner menus *without* brisket, see pages 228 and 229.

I add quite a bit of water to this recipe because I like a lot of gravy. Oma, I suspect, added less.

Season the brisket on all sides with the salt and pepper to taste. Spread the Garlic Oil all over the brisket, pressing it into the meat.

In a large, heavy 6-quart pot, heat the oil over medium-high heat until hot. Add the onions and cook, stirring, until translucent, about 10 minutes. Add the paprika, and stir until the onion slices are well coated. Lay the seasoned brisket on top of the onions, increase the heat to high, and cook until lightly browned on both sides, about 15 minutes total time.

Add the water to the pot and stir to mix it in. Cover the

1-4-pound first-cut brisket

3 tablespoons coarse kosher salt

Fresh pepper

3 to 4 tablespoons Garlic Oil (page 225)

4 tablespoons flavorless vegetable oil

3 medium onions, sliced

3 tablespoons sweet Hungarian paprika

6 cups water

10 new potatoes, peeled

6 large carrots, peeled

Apple-Horseradish Sauce (page 218)

pot, reduce the heat to low, and cook gently for 1½ hours. The meat should be fork-tender. Remove the brisket to a cutting board, cut into thin slices, and cover with aluminum foil to keep warm.

Add the potatoes and carrots to the pot. Arrange them in the cooking liquid, cover, and cook for 30 minutes, or until they test done when pricked with a fork. Add the sliced brisket back to the pot to reheat briefly in the gravy.

To serve, arrange the sliced brisket in the middle of a large platter. Put the carrots and potatoes around the meat and spoon some of the gravy over all. Serve more of the gravy in a bowl to pass at the table. Serve with the Apple-Horseradish Sauce.

SHOE SHOPPING WITH OMA

One of the outings with Oma that I truly dreaded was when she would take me shoe shopping. She wore the type of shoes grandmothers back then seemed to like: typically black, laces in the front, sturdy, stocky heels. They struck me as clunky for a woman as stylish as Oma was.

We'd start at Macy's. Oma would try on every possible pair, not finding one to her liking. Nothing would fit. Next we'd go to Gimbel's, and it would be the same story. Then, maybe, it would be on to Gertz's. You can imagine what the waiting was like for a young girl. Eventually, after literally hours of looking, she would finally choose a pair, and we would return home.

Years later I realized what those outings with Oma taught me—perseverance. Stay at it, and a pair will eventually fit. It was an excellent lesson for life.

CHOLENT

MAKES AT LEAST 10 GENEROUS SERVINGS

¼ cup *each* dried lima beans, dried chickpeas, dried navy beans, and dried red kidney beans, soaked in one bowl overnight in water to cover

2 pounds flanken, in 2 pieces

2½ tablespoons sugar

Coarse kosher salt and fresh pepper, to taste

About 6 tablespoons flavorless vegetable oil

2 large onions, sliced

3 or 4 medium baking potatoes, peeled and cubed

¼ cup pearl barley

Small piece of cheesecloth, for wrapping the barley and beans

Cholent, a long-cooking stew requiring eighteen to twenty-four hours of cooking time is the traditional Sabbath-day dish in Orthodox homes. How it was made in olden times, in observation of the Sabbath, is interesting. The cook would start the cholent at home on Friday afternoon. Before sundown, when cooking is prohibited, she would take the pot to the local baker, where he would leave it in the oven overnight. On the way home from synagogue the next day, the family would retrieve the pot. A nourishing meal of warm cholent followed. This little bit of history is evocative to me, and I wish I could say that I make cholent that way. But these days, with life as busy as it is, I have enlisted an oven of another kind: A 5½-quart Rival brand Crock-Pot does the job.

The first time I ever had cholent I thought of it as a Jewish cassoulet. Speaking from experience, I know that it does make a lovely luncheon dish: I once prepared it for a surprise-party luncheon, along with a big green salad. I remember our dear friend Judy saying when I served it: "Only here, only at Doris's, will you get cholent!"

A reminder: It's easy to forget about the cheesecloth bag of barley and beans. I've done it myself. Write yourself a note.

❖

Drain the beans and set aside.

Season the flanken with the sugar and salt and a generous amount of pepper; it should be well spiced.

In a skillet, heat 3 tablespoons oil over medium-high heat until hot. Add the onions and cook, stirring, until translucent, about 6 to 10 minutes. With a slotted spatula, remove to a plate and set aside.

Add the remaining oil to the skillet and heat until hot. Add the flanken pieces and sauté on both sides until brown, about 4 minutes per side. Remove to another plate.

Season the potatoes with salt and pepper to taste.

In a 5½-quart Crock-Pot, layer the ingredients. Begin with the onions on the bottom, top with flanken, then potatoes, then beans. Pour in water to cover. Cover the Crock-Pot, turn the heat to high, and bring the liquid to a boil.

While the liquid in the Crock-Pot heats, wrap the barley in a small piece of the cheesecloth. Add the bundle to the boiling mixture. Add salt, if desired. Cover the pot, turn the heat to low, and simmer for 18 to 24 hours, checking from time to time and adding water to the pot if needed.

To serve, remove the cheesecloth bag, cut it open, and add the contents to the stew, stirring until combined.

Serve the cholent directly from the Crock-Pot, or transfer it to a large tureen.

Stuffed Cabbage

FOR THE CABBAGE

1 medium-large head (about 3½ pounds) green cabbage, cored

FOR THE SAUCE

2 cups chopped onions (4 medium)

6 cups chopped ripe tomatoes (6 medium)

4 cups water

1 tablespoon coarse kosher salt

1½ cups dark raisins

½ cup honey

½ cup packed dark brown sugar, plus 3 tablespoons, if desired

½ cup fresh lemon juice (from 4 large lemons)

FOR THE FILLING

2 pounds lean ground beef (preferably a combination of half neck meat and half tenderloin)

1 cup cooked rice, cooled

1 small onion, grated (½ cup)

2 teaspoons coarse kosher salt

Pinch fresh pepper, to taste

These cabbage rolls hold a special place in my heart. Oma would always make them for Succoth, when she would serve them either with rice or small boiled potatoes, or Challah (page 58), and her green salad, always her green salad (page 160). It was a fall meal that filled the house with unforgettable aromas. What I remember especially loving about these stuffed rolls, and it is something I still love, is their sweetness. Lots of dark raisins and dark brown sugar make the sauce truly delicious. These get even better as they stand. They also freeze well.

The tradition of serving stuffed cabbage on Succoth continues: My daughter Dena now makes it. She also builds a succah, something I did, too, when we lived on Long Island. Succoth is a wonderful holiday, a celebration of the harvest, and when my children were growing up I used to love to have a Succoth party, with lots of friends invited, pony rides for the children, and klezmer music for all. And, of course, stuffed cabbage.

❖

Blanch the cabbage: Fill an 8-quart soup pot with water, add the cabbage, and bring to a boil over medium-high heat. Simmer for about 30 minutes, or until the leaves wilt. Remove the cabbage from the pot and drain well in a colander. When the cabbage is cool enough to handle, remove the outer leaves and reserve them. One by one, remove the inner leaves, separating them and laying out, rib side down, on the counter for filling. Pat dry with paper towels.

Make the sauce: While the cabbage is cooling, combine the onions, tomatoes, water, and salt in a large, wide saucepan, and bring to a boil over medium-high heat. Add the raisins, ½ cup brown sugar, and lemon juice, and continue to simmer the sauce gently while making the filling and stuffing the leaves.

Make the filling: In a large bowl, combine all the filling ingredients, being careful not to overmix.

Make the rolls: In the center of each cabbage leaf, spoon about 2½ tablespoons of the filling. Bring each of the leaf corners in to cover the filling, then roll the leaf up. As you finish each roll, lay it seam-side down in the simmering sauce.

When all the rolls are in the saucepan, arrange the reserved cabbage leaves on top, covering the rolls. Cover the pan and cook the rolls over low heat for about 2 hours total time, starting from when you put the first rolls in the sauce.

After 1½ hours, remove the cabbage leaves that cover the rolls and discard. Taste the sauce and add up to 3 tablespoons of the remaining brown sugar if you prefer it sweeter. Serve the rolls with plenty of sauce spooned over the top.

FLEISCHLABEL

(*Chopped Meat Patties*)

MAKES 6 OR 7 SERVINGS

1½ pounds lean ground beef
(preferably a combination of
half neck meat and half
tenderloin)

1 small onion, grated

1 extra-large egg

3 tablespoons Homemade
Bread Crumbs (page 62)

1 teaspoon minced garlic

1½ tablespoons chopped fresh
parsley plus additional, for
serving

Coarse kosher salt and fresh
pepper, to taste

Flavorless vegetable oil, for
brushing the patties

For a sophisticated Viennese woman, Oma had simple tastes when it came to food. Among the cherished few dishes she counted as favorites were these meat patties. She used to fry them in oil in a skillet on top of the stove. I broil them instead. The best accompaniment—and the most typical, I'm told—is *Kartoffelpuree* (Mashed Potatoes, page 133), and that is how I have always served them, inspired, like so many other things, by the way Oma did it.

In a bowl, gently combine all the ingredients with your hands, being careful not to overmix. Divide the meat mixture into 7 equal-sized round patties and place them in a single layer on a large plate. Cover with plastic wrap and chill until ready to cook.

Place an oven rack about 3 inches from the heat source and preheat the broiler.

Arrange the beef patties on a broiler pan, and brush the top of each with a little oil. Broil for 4 minutes. With a spatula, turn the patties over and broil for an additional 4 minutes for medium. Transfer the patties to a small serving platter, sprinkle with a little chopped parsley, and serve.

At Home with Oma

An average day for Oma when we lived in Queens took her to several markets, then back home—all on foot. She'd unpack the groceries and immediately start to prepare the evening meal. I can remember thinking how long it took her to do all this; the amount of work and time that was involved impressed me.

Once dinner was over, I would clear the table and do the dishes; you would have thought that after the distances Oma had covered and the amount of standing on her feet she had done that day that she'd want to relax. No, she went out again, to night school to learn English, something she worked hard at. And she walked there, too.

MEAT KABOBS

MAKES 8 SERVINGS

2 pounds lean ground beef
(a combination of half neck
meat and half tenderloin)

6 tablespoons chopped fresh
parsley

¼ cup finely chopped onion

2 teaspoons minced garlic

2 teaspoons coarse kosher salt

Scant ½ teaspoon ground
turmeric

¼ teaspoon ground cumin

When my children were young, I used to make a variation of these kabobs—seasoned ground beef shaped into ovals—as a weeknight supper. The memory of these kabobs came back to me when I began working on this book, and I am happy to report that the recipe has held up well, especially with the addition of turmeric and cumin.

The ovals are small, so if you are serving them as the entrée allow two per person; if you are pairing them with another main dish, as I did with *Backhendl* (Fried Chicken, Viennese Style, page 107) one evening, one is enough. The recipe halves perfectly. You can also barbecue the kabobs. I have occasionally made them with equal parts ground chicken and ground turkey, and that combination works nicely, too.

◆

In a bowl, combine all the ingredients with your hands, taking care not to overmix. Shape into ovals, each about 2 inches long and 1 inch thick. (You should have 18 "kabobs.")

Heat a large ridged grill pan over high heat until hot. Add the kabobs in a single layer, without crowding, and cook, turning often with two forks, until well browned on the outside, but rare within, about 8 minutes total. Transfer to a platter and serve at once.

Meat Loaf

This is a grandmother's recipe, too, but it is not mine, or my mother's, or Oma's. I inherited it from my dear friend Marsha's mother, Rose. The preparation is a little unusual: The loaf cooks surrounded by vegetables in a tomato sauce. Vary the vegetables according to the season and number of guests. And be sure to make the loaf ahead of time and then let it rest. This allows it to slice well.

Even cold, this meat is good, especially in sandwiches.

❖

Preheat the oven to 350 degrees F.

In a large bowl, combine the meat, bread crumbs, grated onion, grated potatoes and carrot, garlic, parsley, salt and pepper to taste, and 1 cup Tomato Sauce, using your hands. Halve the mixture and form each half into a loaf. Put the loaves in a 14 × 10-inch lasagne pan or baking pan of similar size. Scatter the chopped potatoes and onion and the sliced carrots into the pan around the loaves.

In a large measuring cup, combine the water and the remaining 1 cup Tomato Sauce and pour over the loaves and vegetables. Cover the pan tightly with foil.

Bake for 1 hour. Remove the foil, baste the loaves with the pan juices, and bake 1 hour more. (If the liquid in the pan bakes off, add a little water to prevent scorching.) Remove from the oven and let rest for at least 15 minutes before slicing.

2 pounds lean ground beef (preferably a combination of half neck meat and half tenderloin)

½ cup plain fresh Homemade Bread Crumbs (page 62) or plain store-bought crumbs

1 cup grated onion (1 medium)*

1 cup grated, peeled baking potato (1 small to medium)*

¾ cup grated, peeled carrot (about 3 medium)*

2 tablespoons finely chopped garlic

3 tablespoons chopped fresh parsley

2 cups Tomato Sauce (page 221), or store-bought sauce

Coarse kosher salt and fresh pepper, to taste

2 Idaho potatoes, peeled and cut into chunks

1 large onion, coarsely chopped

2 carrots, peeled and sliced

1 cup water

To serve, cut the loaves into slices and serve with the vegetables on the side.

*Note: Grate on the small holes of a handheld box grater for the appropriate texture.

Stuffed Peppers

MAKES 6 PEPPERS

Peppers and paprika are part of the culinary heritage I grew up on, and this dish has both. I sometimes stir steamed green beans into the tomato sauce around the peppers, and I like to serve them with additional white rice and cauliflower florets.

Start checking the peppers after 1 hour of cooking. I cook them another 30 minutes, because I like them collapsed.

Preheat the oven to 350 degrees F.

Rinse the peppers and pat them dry. Cut the top off each pepper, and reserve. Working carefully, core the peppers and remove all the seeds and any thick ribs. Do not puncture the sides of the peppers.

In a bowl, combine well the meat, rice, 2 tablespoons of the parsley, onion, garlic, and paprika, and season with salt and pepper to taste.

Divide the meat filling among the peppers, and lightly press the reserved tops in place.

Pour 1 cup Tomato Sauce into a small roasting pan with sides or casserole. Stir in the water and the remaining 1 tablespoon parsley. Set the stuffed peppers upright in the pan. Scatter the potatoes and carrots into the pan around the peppers. Pour the remaining 1 cup Tomato Sauce over

6 medium red or green bell peppers

1 pound chopped meat, such as lean ground beef or chicken

¾ cup cooked white rice, cooled

3 tablespoons chopped fresh parsley

½ cup chopped onion

1 teaspoon minced garlic

2 tablespoons sweet Hungarian paprika

Coarse kosher salt and fresh pepper, to taste

2 cups Tomato Sauce (page 221) or store-bought sauce

1 cup water

4 new potatoes, peeled and halved

1 carrot, peeled and cut into julienne strips

the peppers. Cover the pan tightly with foil and bake for
I to I½ hours, testing the peppers after I hour.

To serve, arrange the peppers on a serving platter,
spoon the sauce and vegetables around them, and serve.

Beef Goulash with Carrots and Potatoes

MAKES 6 TO 8 SERVINGS

Oma made a lot of stewed meat, reminiscent, I suspect, of the dishes she had made when she lived in Vienna. This goulash is a variation on her Brisket (page 69). It is both comforting and filling, a wonderful everyday dinner.

❖

Season the meat with salt and pepper. Put the flour in a resealable plastic bag, add the seasoned beef, and toss to lightly coat. Remove to a plate.

Heat the oil in a large, heavy pot over medium-high heat until hot. Add the onions, and cook, stirring, until translucent. Add the garlic, and cook, stirring, until fragrant, about 1 minute. Sprinkle in the paprika, and cook, stirring, until the onions are completely coated. Add the beef, in batches, if necessary, and sauté until lightly browned on all sides.

Add the tomato and marjoram and stir to combine. Pour in the water, add the tomato paste, and stir until the tomato paste dissolves. Increase the heat to high and bring the liquid to a boil. Cover the pot, reduce the heat to low, and simmer the stew gently for 1½ hours, stirring occasionally, until the meat is fork-tender.

While the goulash cooks, parboil the potatoes in a medium saucepan in water to cover until just fork-tender, 10 to 15 minutes. Drain, let cool, and peel. Reserve.

2 pounds beef stew meat, preferably chuck, cut into 2-inch pieces

Coarse kosher salt and fresh pepper, to taste

3 tablespoons all-purpose flour

2 to 3 tablespoons flavorless vegetable oil

3 cups chopped onions (about 4)

1 tablespoon chopped garlic

3 tablespoons sweet Hungarian paprika

1 cup chopped tomatoes (2 medium)

1 tablespoon fresh marjoram, or 1 teaspoon dried

3 cups water

1 tablespoon tomato paste

4 medium red potatoes

5 medium carrots, peeled and cut into chunks

At the same time, parboil the carrots in another saucepan of boiling salted water until just fork-tender, about 15 minutes, depending upon their size. Drain and reserve.

When the meat tests fork-tender, add the carrots to the stew and cook over medium-low heat for 20 minutes. Add the potatoes, being sure to cover them with the sauce in the pot, and cook until heated through, 15 to 18 minutes. As the potatoes heat, check to make sure that there is enough liquid in the pot to prevent scorching; if not, add water or beef broth.

Shell Steak with Onions

MAKES 6 TO 8 SERVINGS

My grandmother did the cooking in our household because my mother and my aunt both went to work every day. Even so, my mother made a few recipes, and they are etched in my memory. This is one of them. She liked to call this "potted" meat, because that's how it cooks, in a pot. (It is not to be confused with the English term that identifies certain ingredients, like meat, preserved in a pot or covered jar.)

The cut of meat alone makes this entrée unforgettable. Add potato dumplings, or steamed fingerling potatoes, and a green vegetable, or Perfect Green Bean Salad (page 87), and the meal will be forever etched in your memory, too.

❖

In a large skillet, heat the oil over medium-high heat until hot. Add the onions and cook, stirring, until translucent. Add the garlic and cook, stirring, just until fragrant. Add the paprika and stir until the onions and garlic are completely coated. Stir in the marjoram.

Pat the pieces of steak dry with paper towels, season with salt and pepper, and add to the onion mixture in the skillet. Cook, turning the pieces, until brown on all sides. Pour in the water, stir to blend, and cover the pan. Cook for 1 to 1½ hours, or until the meat is fork-tender. With a

5 tablespoons flavorless vegetable oil

3 cups chopped onions (4 large)

2 teaspoons minced garlic

3 tablespoons sweet Hungarian paprika

1 teaspoon dried marjoram

2½ pounds shell steak, cut into pieces 2 inches long, 1 inch wide, and ¼ inch thick

Coarse kosher salt and fresh pepper, to taste

2 cups water

4 medium carrots, peeled

Potato Dumplings, optional (page 139)

Chopped fresh parsley, for the optional dumplings

slotted spoon, remove the meat to a plate and keep warm, loosely covered with foil.

Add the carrots to the gravy in the skillet and cook for 15 to 20 minutes, or until tender when tested with a fork. If you are serving potato dumplings, add them to the skillet, spooning the gravy over them. Return the meat to the pan and stir gently to combine, being careful not to break up the dumplings. Reduce the heat to medium-low and cook, stirring gently every now and then, just until the dumplings are heated through, from 5 to 8 minutes.

To serve, spoon the meat and gravy into the middle of a platter with sides. Arrange the potato dumplings and carrots decoratively around the meat. Garnish the dumplings with the parsley, if desired. Serve at once.

The Perfect Green Bean Salad

(Serve with Shell Steak with Onions)

MAKES 4 SERVINGS

Sometimes you chance upon the ideal pairing of flavors and textures and colors, and when you find one of those perfect combinations, it is worth remembering. So it is with this salad when you serve it with Shell Steak with Onions (page 85). Try it and see if you don't agree.

Cook the beans as directed on page 172. Drain well.

Transfer the beans to a serving bowl and add the hot broth, tossing to combine. Let stand until cooled to room temperature. Add the onion, vinegar, and olive oil, and toss well to combine. Season with salt and pepper to taste, toss again, and serve.

1 pound green beans, ends trimmed
½ to ¾ cup hot chicken broth
1 very small white onion, thinly sliced
1 tablespoon balsamic vinegar
3 tablespoons olive oil
Coarse kosher salt and fresh pepper, to taste

BUON APPETITO

To this day, some of the warmest memories I have are of the years my family—my mother, father, and me—lived in Italy. I was a baby when we arrived in the small country town of Guardiagrele in the Abruzzi region. We were interned there until I was five, by which time I had come to know a young woman I have never forgotten. Her name was Rosalia, and she had been born in the town. Her family lived there, in a house not far from where we were living. Every day Rosalia cooked for her family, both lunch and dinner. Many times, I was invited to eat with them. Those were happy times around Rosalia's table. Decades later, I learned that Rosalia was not only feeding me, but she was also keeping a watchful eye over me all those years, protecting me from harm's way.

A long flash forward: It is August 2000, and my husband, Marvin, and I are on vacation with my daughter Renée and her husband, Peter, in Italy. We have just finished a cooking class, given in the kitchen of a singular Tuscan farmhouse, and are about to sit down to what we have just made—fried zucchini flowers, pasta with fresh tomato sauce, stuffed tomatoes, fried green tomatoes, a salad of just-picked lettuces and vegetables—at a table on the veranda. Tuft-colored rolling hills stretch for as far as the eye can see. The sky is an indigo blue. Fruit trees bloom. There are big pots of fresh sage and basil and baskets of deep-purple eggplants on the veranda. We sit down at the table as a family, with Maria and her husband, owners of the farm, their daughter Roberta, the village priest, and our guide, Silvio. That luncheon and long afternoon of camaraderie, wholesome food, and slanting sunlight rekindled something in me, touched memories I had been holding deep within. One word sums up that day for me: happiness.

Another flash forward, but only several years this time. Again, it is summer, and we are—where else?—in Italy. But this time, my sister, Ruth, and my granddaughter Sara have joined Marvin and me. I am determined that Ruth, who was born in a barn in Guardiagrele, savor the experience of a visit to the magical farmhouse in Tuscany. Years had passed, but Maria is there, once again she shares her culinary know-how with us, and as I had hoped, we sit down to another summer feast on the veranda.

Some things never change, nor do you want them to. Such is my attachment to, and affinity for, Italy.

WIENER SCHNITZEL

(Viennese Veal Cutlets)

MAKES 10 SERVINGS

Oma made these wonderful cutlets as an everyday dinner. She would buy the meat at the butcher in pieces that were much bigger than the cutlets we have today. She paired these with Parsleyed Potatoes (page 132) and Cucumber Salad (page 166). Everything about the dinner was good.

❖

Pat the cutlets dry with paper towels and season with salt and pepper on both sides.

Spread the flour on a large plate.

In a wide, shallow bowl, beat the eggs with salt and pepper to taste until combined.

Spread the bread crumbs in an even layer on a large plate.

Prepare the cutlets: One at a time, dredge each cutlet in the flour, shaking off the excess. Dip the cutlets into the beaten eggs, letting any extra drip back into the bowl, and finally, coat the cutlet on both sides in the crumbs. Lay the cutlets as they are breaded in a single layer on a large plate. Cover the plate with plastic wrap and put it in the refrigerator until cooking time.

Preheat the oven to 200 degrees F.

10 kosher veal medallions, cut from the shoulder, each ¼ inch thick

Coarse kosher salt and fresh pepper, to taste

Flour, for dredging

4 extra-large eggs, beaten lightly

About 1½ cups Homemade Bread Crumbs (page 62)

Flavorless vegetable oil, for cooking

Lemon wedges, for serving

In a large skillet, heat ½ inch oil over medium heat until hot. Add enough cutlets to fit the pan without crowding and cook for 3 to 4 minutes per side, depending upon the thickness, until golden brown. Do not overcook. Arrange the cooked cutlets in a single layer on a baking sheet and keep warm in the preheated oven. Cook the remaining cutlets in the same manner.

Transfer the cutlets to a serving platter, garnish with the lemon wedges, and serve.

Veal Stew with Tomatoes and Green Pepper

MAKES 6 SERVINGS

Whenever I'm making this stew, I find myself thinking the same thing as I lift the lid off the pot to add the potatoes: "It smells exactly like Oma's." The combination of slow-cooked onions, garlic, sweet paprika, tomatoes, and bell peppers create the singular taste.

Pat the veal pieces dry with paper towels and season with salt and pepper to taste.

In a heavy 5-quart stew pot, heat the oil over medium heat until hot. Add the onions and garlic and cook, stirring, about 10 minutes, until the onions are lightly colored. Add the paprika and stir in with a wooden spoon, making sure that it is well incorporated into the onion mixture.

Add the seasoned veal to the pot, and stir to coat the veal with the onion mixture. Cover the pot tightly and reduce the heat to medium-low. Simmer the veal for 20 to 30 minutes, stirring occasionally.

Stir in the chopped tomatoes, cover the pot, and cook for 15 minutes. Stir in the green pepper and simmer, stir-

3 pounds shoulder of veal, cut into 1½-inch pieces

Coarse kosher salt and fresh pepper, to taste

6 tablespoons flavorless vegetable oil

3 cups chopped onions (4 large)

3 teaspoons chopped garlic

2 tablespoons sweet Hungarian paprika

3 cups chopped peeled tomatoes (4 large)

1 medium green bell pepper, cored, seeds and ribs removed, and chopped (1 cup)

Boiled potatoes (page 132), drained and still hot, *not* sprinkled with chopped parsley

3 tablespoons chopped fresh parsley, for garnish

ring occasionally, for 50 minutes, until the veal is fork-tender. Taste the stew and adjust the seasonings.

Add the hot boiled potatoes to the pot, spoon the sauce over them to cover, and simmer over low heat, 5 to 10 minutes, turning them once. Transfer the stew to a serving platter and sprinkle with the chopped parsley.

VEAL STEW WITH MUSHROOMS

MAKES 6 SERVINGS, WITH OTHER ENTRÉES

S tew was a favorite dish of my grandmother's and growing up we had it often, in both beef and veal varieties. Oma would have served broad egg noodles with toasted crumbs as an accompaniment. I have updated that with the choice of bow-tie pasta. Don't omit the crumbs! Either makes just the right side dish.

In a large skillet, heat the oil over medium heat until hot. Add the onions and cook, stirring, until translucent, 6 to 8 minutes. Remove the pan from the heat.

Season the veal with salt, about 2 teaspoons, and pepper to taste. Put the flour in a plastic bag, add the caraway seeds, and shake to combine. Add the veal to the bag in batches, shaking to coat it lightly. Remove the pieces to a plate.

Place the skillet of sautéed onions over medium heat and heat until hot. Add the veal and stir to coat the pieces with the oil and onions. Cover the skillet with a tight-fitting lid, reduce the heat to low, and cook 5 to 8 minutes, shaking the pan occasionally to prevent the veal from sticking.

Stir in the water, broth, and mushrooms. Cover the skillet and simmer the mixture gently, still over low heat, until the veal is fork-tender, about 1 hour, checking

4 tablespoons flavorless vegetable oil, or more as needed

2 cups chopped onions (3 large)

2 pounds shoulder of veal, cut into 2-inch pieces

Coarse kosher salt and fresh pepper, to taste

2 to 3 tablespoons all-purpose flour

1 tablespoon caraway seeds

1 cup water

1 cup chicken broth, or more as needed

4 cups sliced shiitake mushrooms

occasionally to make sure that there is liquid in the bottom of the skillet. If not, add water or broth, a tablespoon at a time.

Transfer the stew to a serving platter.

Veal Roast with Roasted Fresh Vegetables

MAKES 8 TO 10 SERVINGS

This is an extravagant dish, full of flavor and very tender. It's suitable for a special occasion, though it isn't hard to prepare. For the best results, have a meat thermometer on hand and check it regularly as the suggested cooking time winds down. This is a superb dish for a holiday meal; for a Rosh Hashanah menu, see page 237.

Preheat the oven to 375 degrees F.

Season the roast: Coarsely chop the sage leaves with thyme leaves. In a small bowl, combine the chopped herbs with a scant tablespoon of salt, and 5 or 6 grindings of pepper. Sprinkle the mixture over the roast, then press it on with your hands. Rub the Garlic Oil all over the roast. Transfer the roast to a medium roasting pan with low sides and grind coarse black pepper over the top.

Put the cut-up vegetables in the pan around the roast, then pour the broth over them.

Roast the veal on the middle rack of the oven for about 1½ hours. A meat thermometer will ensure perfect doneness: It should register a minimum of 170 degrees F for medium (160 to 165 degrees F = rare; and 180 degrees F = well done).

5 fresh sage leaves

1 tablespoon fresh thyme leaves

Coarse kosher salt and fresh pepper, to taste

1 5-pound rack of veal, filleted and tied with kitchen string

¼ cup Garlic Oil (page 225)

2 large Idaho potatoes, peeled and cut into chunks

2 large carrots, peeled and cut into thick slices

1 large onion, coarsely chopped

4 stalks celery, with leaves, cut into 1-inch pieces

2 cups chicken broth

Remove the roast to a platter and tent it closely with foil to keep it warm.

Return the pan of vegetables to the oven and roast about 30 minutes longer, until the broth has cooked off and the vegetables have turned a deep, rich brown and the onions are caramelized on the edges.

To serve, remove the strings from the roast and slice it into even pieces, arranging them on the platter. Cut the racks on which the veal was tied into individual ribs, and arrange them on the platter as tasty morsels. Serve the roasted vegetables alongside, or as a separate dish.

CALVES' LIVER WITH APPLES AND ONIONS

MAKES 4 SERVINGS

When I served this to friends at a small weeknight dinner, with steamed cauliflower and parsleyed fingerling potatoes, there was not a thing left on the platter. Do not be tempted to use anything but calves' liver, and ask the butcher to slice it almost paper thin.

Preheat the oven to 200 degrees F.

In a medium skillet, heat 2 tablespoons of the oil over medium heat until hot. Add the onions and salt to taste, and cook, stirring constantly, until translucent and softened but not browned, about 10 minutes. (You must stir the onions continuously to achieve the best texture.) Remove with a slotted spoon to a heatproof bowl and keep warm in the preheated oven.

Rinse out the skillet, and dry it well. Heat the margarine in the skillet until melted, add the apple rings, and cook, turning them gently, until softened, about 7 minutes. Remove with the slotted spoon to another heatproof bowl and keep warm in the oven.

Spread flour out on a plate. Dredge the liver, one piece at a time, in the flour, coating it well and shaking off any excess.

In a large skillet, heat the remaining 4 tablespoons oil until hot. Add the liver slices in a single layer, and cook

6 tablespoons flavorless vegetable oil

3 medium onions, cut into thin slices, then separated into rings

Coarse kosher salt, to taste

2 tablespoons unsalted margarine

5 or 6 McIntosh apples, peeled, cored, and sliced crosswise into ¼-inch-thick rings

Flour, for dredging

6 very thin slices calves' liver (almost 2 pounds), cut barely ¼ inch thick by the butcher

over high heat until just browned, about 2 minutes. Turn the slices over and cook for 2 to 3 minutes for rare. (Test for doneness by cutting into one of the slices. The meat should be pink. Do not overcook.) Remove the slices immediately to a large platter and on one end of it spoon the onions and on the other arrange the apple rings. Serve at once.

POULTRY

Orange-Glazed Chicken

MAKES 6 TO 8 SERVINGS

3 to 3¼ pounds (8 pieces)
  kosher chicken
2 teaspoons sweet Hungarian
  paprika
Pinch fresh pepper

FOR THE MARINADE
1 cup orange juice
⅓ cup soy sauce
⅓ cup orange marmalade
¼ cup ketchup

Here is one of the dishes I serve at Friday-night dinners for my family (see page 228). I must say, everyone loves it. There is never a piece of chicken left. The assembly is easy and involves a marinade of everyday ingredients, then simple baking the next day.

Substitute apricot preserves for the orange marmalade if you like apricots as much as I do.

Season the chicken with the paprika and pepper, then put the pieces in a shallow pan.

Make the marinade: In a bowl, whisk together all of the marinade ingredients, stirring until the marmalade is dissolved.

Pour the marinade over the chicken, and turn to coat the pieces well. Cover the pan with plastic wrap, and refrigerate overnight.

Preheat the oven to 350 degrees F.

Drain the chicken and discard the marinade. Arrange the chicken on a large baking sheet and bake for 1½ hours.

Transfer the chicken to a platter and serve hot, or cooled to warm.

Roast Chicken with Bread Stuffing

MAKES 3 TO 4 SERVINGS

Oma made roast chicken often, with or without stuffing, and I still have the enamel roasting pan she made it in.

Here is how I prepare the chicken when I don't have time to make the stuffing: Season the cavity well with salt and pepper, then stuff it with 8 garlic cloves, peeled, and 1 small onion, peeled and left whole. Season the outside of the chicken as directed below and roast for the same amount of time.

Make the stuffing: In a large skillet, heat the oil over medium-high heat until hot. Add the onion, celery, and garlic, stirring to combine, and cook until the onion pieces are translucent, about 5 minutes. Add the bread cubes and stir to combine. Add the broth and stir until the cubes are thoroughly moistened. Add the parsley and stir to combine. Remove the pan from the heat and let the stuffing cool completely.

Preheat the oven to 400 degrees F.

Prepare the chicken: Rub the chicken all over with the salt and pepper to taste. Salt and pepper the chicken cavity as well. Spread the Garlic Oil all over the chicken, pressing it firmly into the skin. Lastly, rub the paprika into the skin.

When the stuffing is completely cooled, stuff the cavity

FOR THE STUFFING
2 tablespoons flavorless
  vegetable oil
1 cup chopped onion (1 large)
1 cup chopped celery
1 garlic clove, chopped
2 cups stale bread cubes or
  croutons
1½ cups chicken broth or
  Chicken Soup (page 40)
1 tablespoon chopped fresh
  parsley

FOR THE CHICKEN
1 3-pound kosher chicken
1½ tablespoons coarse kosher
  salt
Fresh pepper, to taste
2 tablespoons Garlic Oil
  (page 225)
1 tablespoon sweet Hungarian
  paprika

and neck of the chicken. If desired, use a heel of bread to cover the cavity opening. Put the chicken in a small roasting pan, cover with the lid or foil, and roast for 1 hour. Remove the cover or foil, reduce the heat to 350 degrees F, and roast for 15 to 20 minutes, until the skin is golden brown in color.

Remove the chicken to platter and carve. Serve with the stuffing.

My Mother's Chicken Paprika

MAKES 6 SERVINGS

Here is another of my mother's recipes, which my sister has made over the years as well. It is chicken paprika, *without* the sour cream, but with a most wonderful sauce of its own. My mother served this with Risi Bisi (page 148); Brown Rice with Mushrooms (page 150) would be another excellent choice.

Pour the flour into a resealable plastic bag and season with salt and pepper to taste. One piece at a time, dredge the chicken in the flour mixture, coating it on all sides. Shake off the excess and put the chicken in a single layer on a plate.

In a large deep skillet or sauté pan (11 to 12 inches wide), heat the oil over medium-high heat until hot. In batches, add the chicken in a single layer, without crowding, and cook until very lightly browned on both sides, about several minutes per side. Remove with tongs to a large plate.

Add the onions to the oil in the pan and sauté them, stirring occasionally, until translucent. Stir in the paprika until the onion pieces are well coated. Add the garlic, and cook just until fragrant. Add the broth and bring to a boil. Return the chicken to the pan and turn it to coat it with the onions. Arrange the chicken skin side down,

About 1½ cups all-purpose flour, for dredging

Coarse kosher salt and fresh pepper, to taste

3 pounds kosher frying chicken, cut into pieces

3 tablespoons flavorless vegetable oil

2 cups chopped onions, red or white (2 large)

1½ tablespoons sweet Hungarian paprika

1 tablespoon chopped garlic

2 cups chicken broth or Chicken Soup (page 40)

bring the broth back to a boil, and cover the pan. Lower the heat and simmer gently for 1 hour, turning the pieces every now and then, until the chicken is cooked through.

Transfer the chicken and sauce to a platter, and serve with Risi Bisi or plain white rice.

MY CHICKEN CUTLETS

MAKES 6 SERVINGS

"Grandma, please make your chicken cutlets." That says it all.

I could never make enough of these for my own family. Food in my house disappeared. There was never any junk food. I will never forget the time when I was playing cards over lunch one day. My sons were downstairs playing pool with a group of friends. It was only after the card game that I learned they'd opened up the freezer, helped themselves to the steaks in it, thawed them quickly, and cooked them on the grill. No junk food? No problem, there was steak!

These are wonderful served right out of the pan. If you double the recipe, which is easy to do, keep the first batch of cooked cutlets warm in a low (200-degree F oven) while you cook the second batch. Or, serve these at room temperature, buffet style, with a selection of salads.

Flour, for dredging (about 1 cup)

2 extra-large eggs, beaten lightly, with 1 of the egg shell halves reserved

Water or seltzer (a tablespoon more or less)

3 tablespoons chopped fresh chives

Coarse kosher salt and fresh pepper, to taste

About 1½ cups Homemade Bread Crumbs (page 62)

1 pound skinless, boneless chicken breasts (3 pieces)

Juice of ½ lemon

Flavorless vegetable oil, for frying

Spread the flour on a wide, shallow plate.

In a wide, shallow plate with sides (a pie plate, for example), beat the egg together with enough water or seltzer to fill the reserved egg shell. Stir in the chives and salt and pepper to taste.

Spread the bread crumbs out on a large plate.

With a sharp knife, slice each of the chicken breasts horizontally through the middle to make 2 thinner pieces.

Wipe the chicken pieces with the lemon juice, rinse, and pat dry with paper towels.

Bread the chicken cutlets by dipping them, one at a time, first into the flour; shake off the excess. Next, dip the cutlet into the beaten eggs, coating it well and pressing the chives on with your hand. Then dredge the cutlet in the bread crumbs, shaking off any excess crumbs. Reserve the breaded cutlets on a plate.

Heat enough oil to generously glaze the bottom of a large skillet over medium-high heat until hot. Add the cutlets in a single layer, and cook until golden, about 4 minutes. Turn and cook until golden on the second side, again about 4 minutes. Transfer the cutlets with tongs to paper towels to drain briefly, and serve hot. Or let cool and serve at room temperature.

BACKHENDL

(Fried Chicken, Viennese Style)

MAKES 8 TO 10 SERVINGS

My husband, Marvin, loves fried chicken, and when we lived on Long Island our neighbor and dear friend Susan, had a wonderful family helper, Sarah. She was from the Deep South and she made the best fried chicken in the world. It was so extraordinary that Marvin used to go over and watch Sarah make it. Marvin, whose opinion I trust, especially about fried chicken, says that this version is very good, too.

Unlike this recipe, Sarah did not dip her chicken into crumbs, only seasoned flour. She also added a whole onion to the hot oil for flavoring, and while that is not what my Viennese relatives would have done, I include it here because it is such a nice touch. Otherwise this is the way Oma prepared it. This recipe makes a lot, but is there such a thing as too much good fried chicken? Marvin doesn't think so.

❖

½ cup fresh lemon juice (3 large)

1 3½-pound kosher chicken, cut into 8 pieces, plus 2 whole chicken breasts, halved

Coarse kosher salt and fresh pepper, to taste

Flour, for dredging (about 1½ cups)

About 3 cups Homemade Bread Crumbs (page 62)

Flavorless vegetable oil, for deep-frying

4 extra-large eggs, beaten lightly

½ cup seltzer or water

1 small onion, optional, peeled

Pour the lemon juice into a wide shallow ceramic or glass plate (a pie plate works well) and add the chicken. Turn each piece to cover completely with the lemon juice. Let stand at room temperature for at least 15 minutes. Remove the chicken and pat it dry with paper towels. Season with salt and pepper to taste.

While the chicken marinates, put enough flour for dredging the chicken in a resealable plastic food storage bag. Put enough bread crumbs to coat the chicken in another large resealable plastic bag.

In a high-sided large (6-quart) pot, heat enough oil to measure 1 inch over medium-high heat until very hot.

In a medium bowl, whisk the beaten eggs with the seltzer until well combined.

Drop the chicken, a few pieces at a time, into the flour, dredging it well. Shake off any excess flour, and put the pieces as they are floured on a large plate in a single layer.

Dip the chicken, a few pieces at a time, into the beaten egg mixture, coating them completely.

Finally, drop each piece, into the bread crumbs, dredging it well and making sure it is completely coated. Place the chicken on a platter or baking sheet in a single layer.

Preheat the oven to 200 degrees F. Line a large baking sheet with paper towels.

Test the oil for hotness: Drop a cube of bread into the heated oil. If bubbles instantly pop up around the cube, the oil is hot enough for deep-frying. Scoop out the bread cube with a slotted spoon, then carefully ease as many pieces as will fit into the pan without crowding. Add the onion, if desired. Partially cover the pot and fry the chicken, turning it often with long-handled tongs, for 10 to 15 minutes, until crisp and golden brown in color. (Remove the white meat sooner than the dark, and take care not to overcook the dark.) Put the pieces on the lined baking sheet to drain briefly. Remove the paper towels, and transfer the sheet to the preheated oven. Fry and drain the remaining chicken in the same manner.

Serve hot, warm, or at room temperature. This chicken is also wonderful cold the next day.

APRICOT-STUFFED CHICKEN BREASTS

MAKES 8 SERVINGS

I was inspired to make this recipe when chicken Kiev was so popular—the allure being the discovery of an unexpected taste inside the gently sauteed chicken. The meat is exceptionally tender, and the apricot filling is surprising and different. If you are fortunate enough to have apricots in brandy, use them for the plain apricot halves called for below. Serve with Risi Bisi (page 148).

For a complete Friday night dinner menu that features this dish, see page 229.

❖

Season the flattened chicken breasts with salt and pepper to taste on both sides. Put 1 or 2 small apricot halves, pit side up, in the middle of 1 of the halves of each breast. Sprinkle with ¼ teaspoon each of minced garlic and chopped chives, then place 1 tablespoon of the margarine on top of the apricots. Fold the seasoned half of the breast to cover the apricot filling and press down firmly with the palm of your hand to seal. Stuff the remaining breasts in the same manner.

Whisk the eggs together again in a wide, shallow dish to recombine.

Spread the flour in an even layer on a plate and season with salt and pepper to taste.

8 skinless, boneless whole chicken breasts, pounded with a mallet until ⅛ inch thick

Coarse kosher salt and fresh pepper, to taste

1 can (16 ounces) apricot halves in juice, drained

2 teaspoons minced garlic

2 teaspoons minced chives, plus additional for garnish

8 tablespoons (1 stick) unsalted margarine, cut into 8 pieces

2 extra-large eggs, beaten lightly

About 1½ cups all-purpose flour, for dredging

2 cups Homemade Bread Crumbs (page 62)

Flavorless vegetable oil, for frying

Pour the bread crumbs onto a large plate, season with salt and pepper to taste, and spread in an even layer.

One at a time, carefully dredge the chicken breasts in the flour and shake off the excess. Dip in the eggs, and lastly dredge in the bread crumbs, coating completely and pressing the crumbs on. Take care to keep the chicken breasts firmly sealed. (If you need to, seal the edges with a little extra egg and crumbs, or insert wooden toothpicks to keep them closed.) Put the breaded chicken in a single layer on a large plate, cover tightly with plastic wrap, and refrigerate for 1 hour.

Preheat the oven to 200 degrees F. Line a baking sheet with paper towels.

Heat ½ to ¾ inch oil in a large skillet over medium-high heat until hot when tested with a bread cube. (If bubbles instantly pop up around the bread cube, the oil is ready.) Carefully add the chicken breasts, a few at a time, and fry them, turning frequently, until golden brown, 8 to 10 minutes. With a slotted spoon, remove the chicken to the baking sheet to drain briefly. Remove the paper towels and put the baking sheet in the preheated oven. Fry the remaining chicken in the same manner.

Arrange the chicken breasts on a serving platter, sprinkle with the remaining chives, garnishing the platter as well, if desired, and serve at once.

LEMON CHICKEN

MAKES 6 TO 8 SERVINGS

Can there ever be enough recipes for chicken? I don't think so. This is a long-standing favorite of mine, which for some reason I had not made in a while. At a recent family dinner, I brought it out again. I now know why it was something I made often. It was devoured.

Serve with plain rice, as I did for my husband and children, or with Lentil and Rice Pilaf (page 149).

Cut the chicken breasts into ¼-inch-thick strips and put in a bowl.

In a bowl, whisk together the soy sauce, vodka, salt, and ¼ teaspoon oil until combined. Pour the mixture over the chicken, stir to coat, and let stand at room temperature for 30 minutes. Drain and discard the marinade.

Preheat the oven to 200 degrees F.

In a large bowl, beat the egg whites with an electric mixer on medium speed until frothy. Add the drained chicken, stirring to coat, then drain in a colander.

Put the flour in a large resealable plastic bag. Add the chicken strips in batches, dredging them to coat. Shake off the excess, and arrange the strips on a plate in a single layer.

In a large skillet or sauté pan, heat the ⅓ cup oil over medium-high heat until hot. Add the chicken and stir-fry, tossing, until golden brown on all sides, 3 to 4 minutes in a

8 skinless, boneless chicken
    breast halves
2 tablespoons soy sauce
1 tablespoon vodka
1 teaspoon coarse kosher salt
¼ teaspoon plus ⅓ cup flavorless
    vegetable oil
3 extra-large egg whites
1 cup all-purpose flour

FOR THE LEMON SAUCE
¾ cup sugar
½ cup white vinegar
1 cup chicken broth
1 tablespoon cornstarch
    dissolved in 2 tablespoons
    water
Juice and grated zest of
    1 medium lemon
¼ cup slivered blanched
    almonds, for serving

well-heated pan. With a slotted spoon, transfer the chicken to paper towels to drain. Transfer the chicken to a baking sheet and place in the preheated oven to keep warm while you make the sauce.

Make the sauce: In a saucepan, whisk together the sugar, vinegar, broth, cornstarch mixture, and lemon juice and zest. Place the pan over medium heat, and heat, whisking, until the sauce comes to a simmer and thickens.

Arrange the chicken on a serving platter, pour the lemon sauce over it, and scatter the almonds on top. Serve at once.

Pepper Ragout with Sausage

MAKES 6 TO 8 SERVINGS

On one of the many wonderful occasions my Austrian friend Elisabeth Pozzi-Thanner and I were discussing the foods of Vienna, she asked me if Oma or my mother had ever made a dish called *lecsó*, a combination of peppers and tomatoes. In fact, my mother had made a side dish that sounded like it, which my own children had come to love whenever she prepared her "salsa," as she called it, at our house.

In Vienna, Elisabeth said, *lecsó* frequently includes sausage, which then makes it a main course. I discovered that I could buy kosher sausage, and added it to my pepper ragout. The result is outstanding.

Serve with Parsleyed Potatoes (page 132), which are delicious with the sauce. Of course, if you add the optional Yukon potatoes to the pepper ragout, you won't need an accompaniment of boiled potatoes: You will already have made a full main course, including potatoes, in one pot.

Pepper Ragout, made without the Yukon potatoes (page 143)

2 cups Tomato Sauce (page 221)

2 pounds kosher sweet chicken sausage with apple

◆

Heat the Pepper Ragout in a large wide saucepan over medium heat. Stir in the Tomato Sauce and cook, stirring, until the mixture just comes to a simmer.

Add the sausages to the hot ragout, submerging them

completely, and cook over medium-low heat, turning the sausages from time to time and keeping them covered in the sauce, for 30 to 40 minutes, or until cooked through.

Transfer the ragout to a serving platter with sides, and arrange the sausages, cut into smaller pieces, if desired, in the center.

Note: I buy kosher sausages from Park East Kosher Butchers, Inc., 1623 Second Avenue, New York, NY 10028. (212) 737–9800.

Roast Turkey with Apple, Almond, and Raisin Stuffing

MAKES AT LEAST 8 GENEROUS SERVINGS

In my own household, Thanksgiving was always a gala occasion, with Oma, my mother, my sister, Uncle Rudy and Aunt Ciel among the guests.

The way this turkey is prepared, with so many special ingredients in the stuffing, is indicative of how I wanted the holidays in my household to be—truly festive, with family and friends enjoying themselves, with wonderful food, lots of wonderful food, and good times from beginning to end. This turkey and stuffing do not disappoint.

This is a wonderful main course for a dinner for Succoth as well as for Thanksgiving. For a complete menu, including corn bread and cranberry chutney, and much more, see page 242. Should you have turkey left over, you might also want to try my daughter Laura's recipe for Turkey Pot Pie (page 117), which is out of this world.

❖

Make the stuffing: In a wide, large saucepan or sauté pan, heat the oil over medium-high heat until hot. Add the onion, and cook, stirring, until golden. Add the apples and raisins, and cook until the apple pieces color, but do not brown, 4 to 6 minutes. Add the croutons and stir well to combine with the apples and onion. Add the broth,

FOR THE STUFFING
1 small onion, diced
2 tablespoons flavorless vegetable oil
2½ cups peeled, cored, chopped McIntosh apples (3 medium)
½ cup raisins
6 cups plain bread cubes or croutons
6 cups Vegetable Broth (page 51)
¼ cup chopped fresh parsley
1 teaspoon chopped fresh marjoram
¾ cup almonds, toasted and chopped
Coarse kosher salt and pepper, to taste

FOR THE TURKEY
1 10- to 12-pound kosher turkey
Sage and Rosemary Rub (page 224)
2 to 3 tablespoons sweet Hungarian paprika
¼ cup Garlic Oil (page 225)

parsley, and marjoram, and cook to combine and heat through. Remove the pan from the heat, stir in the almonds, and season to taste with salt and pepper. Let cool completely.

Preheat the oven to 450 degrees F. Fit a large roasting pan with a V-rack.

Make the turkey: Rinse the turkey in cold water and pat it dry. Massage the Sage and Rosemary Rub over the outside of the turkey and in the cavity as well, rubbing it in. Dust the turkey all over with the paprika. Lastly, spread the Garlic Oil over the turkey, pressing it into the skin.

When the stuffing is completely cool, pack the turkey cavity and the neck cavity with the stuffing, patting the openings firm. Put the turkey on the rack in the roasting pan and tent the turkey with aluminum foil. Roast for 1 hour.

Lower the temperature to 400 degrees F and roast the turkey for 1 hour more. Remove the foil, baste the turkey with the pan drippings, and carefully rotate the pan in the oven. Roast for 30 minutes more. Test the turkey for doneness by pricking the thigh with a fork or the tip of a sharp knife. If the juices run clear when the thigh is pierced, the turkey is done. (Another sign of doneness is the color of the skin; it should be a rich, golden brown.) Remove the turkey from the oven and transfer it to a serving platter. Tent loosely with foil, if desired, until serving time. Reserve the pan drippings for making the filling for Turkey Pot Pie (page 117).

Carve the turkey, arrange the slices on a large platter, and, if desired, spoon out some of the stuffing alongside.

Turkey Pot Pie

MAKES 6 SERVINGS

Since my oldest daughter, Laura, has five children, she makes sure to put leftovers to good use. She shared this recipe with me, and one thing you should know right off is that it makes a lot of filling: enough for two pot pies. However, since my husband loves turkey à la king, I like to make one pot pie, and serve the remaining turkey mixture over white rice for Marvin and anyone else around the table who is not in the mood for pot pie. (There is enough turkey à la king to serve four.) If you are a fan of pot pie and want to make two pies, remember that you will need to make two batches of dough.

❖

Preheat the oven to 350 degrees F.

Make the dough: In the bowl of an electric mixer fitted with the paddle attachment, blend the flour, margarine, salt, and orange juice on low speed until a ball of dough forms around the paddle. Remove the dough, pat it into a disk, then cut it in half. Wrap one half in plastic wrap and refrigerate until firm.

On a lightly floured surface, roll the dough half into an 11-inch round, roll up around the rolling pin, and center it and unroll over a 10-inch pie plate. Press the dough into plate and up the sides. Double-fold the overhang to reinforce the edge and trim off any extra dough. Line the

FOR THE DOUGH
2 cups all-purpose flour
12 tablespoons (1½ sticks) unsalted margarine, cut into pieces
1 teaspoon coarse kosher salt
5 tablespoons orange juice

FOR THE FILLING
8 tablespoons (1 stick) unsalted margarine
1 teaspoon chopped garlic
1 cup diced onion (1 medium-large)
1 cup diced celery (3 stalks, including the leaves)
1 cup diced peeled carrots (3 or 4 medium)
¼ pound sliced shiitake mushrooms (about 1 cup sliced)
1 teaspoon chopped fresh thyme
½ teaspoon chopped fresh sage leaves
4 cups water
8 tablespoons skimmed-of-fat drippings from Roast Turkey (page 115)
⅔ cup all-purpose flour
1 cup frozen peas
1 cup corn kernels, fresh or frozen
3 cups cubed skinless boneless leftover Roast Turkey (page 115), white and dark meat
1 extra-large egg, beaten lightly with 1 tablespoon water, for egg wash

shell with parchment paper and fill the paper with dried beans or pie weights. Blind-bake the shell for 10 to 15 minutes. Remove the shell from the oven and when cool remove the weights and paper.

Make the filling: In a large skillet, melt 2 tablespoons of the margarine. Add the garlic and sauté, stirring, for 1 minute, until fragrant. Add the onion, celery, carrots, mushrooms, thyme, and sage and cook, stirring, over low heat for 15 minutes, until the vegetables are softened.

While the vegetables cook, in a saucepan, combine the water and skimmed turkey pan drippings. Heat over low heat until just warm. Keep warm while you make the *roux.*

Make the roux: In a large saucepan, melt the remaining 6 tablespoons margarine over low heat. Add the flour and stir to incorporate it completely. Cook, stirring constantly, until the mixture thickens and comes together like a *roux,* or paste, 1 to 2 minutes. Slowly add the warm turkey broth to the pan, whisking constantly to prevent lumps from forming. Bring the mixture to a boil, and cook, whisking occasionally, for about 5 minutes, until thickened and smooth.

Add the sauce to the vegetables in the skillet. Stir in the peas, corn, and turkey and combine well. Taste the filling and adjust the seasonings as desired. (Remember that the turkey was roasted with an herb and salt rub. Do not over-salt the filling.) Remove the pan from the heat while you roll out the top crust.

Lightly reflour the work surface, and roll the remaining piece of dough into an 11-inch round.

Pour one half of the turkey filling into the prebaked pie shell. Reserve the remaining turkey filling, covered and refrigerated, for another use. Roll the dough round gently over the rolling pin, and center it over the filling. Trim the overhang, then crimp the edge of the pie all the way around with the tines of a fork. Brush the top crust and edge lightly with the beaten egg wash. Prick the top of the crust with the fork, and with a small sharp knife cut 4 thin slits in the center as air vents.

Transfer the pie plate to a baking sheet and bake the pie for 20 to 30 minutes, or until the crust is golden brown. Transfer the pot pie to a wire rack and let cool for 5 minutes before serving.

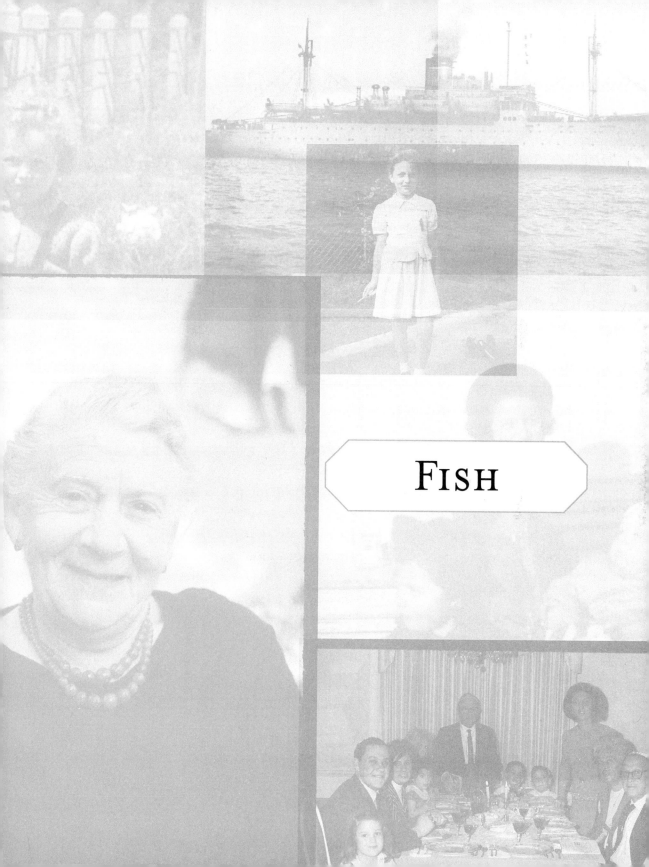

FISH

Fresh Salmon Cakes

MAKES 8 TO 10 CAKES

1½ pounds salmon fillet, skin removed, and fish cut into cubes

½ green bell pepper, chopped

½ red bell pepper, chopped

2 scallions, ends trimmed, green and white parts, chopped

2 tablespoons chopped red onion

1 tablespoon chopped fresh dill

1 tablespoon chopped fresh parsley

2 extra-large eggs, beaten lightly

½ cup Homemade Bread Crumbs (page 62)

Coarse kosher salt and fresh pepper, to taste

Flavorless vegetable oil, for cooking

Cucumber-Dill Sauce (page 219), for serving

If Oma ever made salmon cakes in Vienna, she made them with canned salmon, and now I know why. My Austrian friend Elisabeth explained: "Back then, there was no salmon in Austria. People used fresh carp." You can use carp as a substitute for this recipe, too.

In a food processor fitted with the metal blade, grind the salmon. Add the bell peppers, scallions, red onion, and herbs and pulse several times just to combine. Scrape the mixture into a bowl and stir in the eggs and bread crumbs until well combined. Season with salt and pepper to taste.

Form the salmon mixture into 10 equally sized patties, arranging them in a single layer on a large plate. Cover with plastic wrap and refrigerate for 30 minutes.

Heat a large skillet over medium-high until hot and add enough oil to film the pan bottom. When the oil is hot but not smoking, add as many of the salmon cakes as will fit without crowding the pan and pan-fry them for about 3 to 5 minutes per side, turning when golden brown. With a slotted spatula, transfer the fish cakes to paper towels to drain and keep warm, loosely covered with aluminum foil. Cook and drain the remaining patties in the same manner.

Serve the salmon cakes on a platter, with the Cucumber-Dill Sauce as an accompaniment.

FRIED FLOUNDER

MAKES 6 TO 8 SERVINGS

Sautéing thin fish fillets should be easy, but how often have they fallen apart in the pan as you turned them to cook on the second side? The way these fillets are breaded and then chilled keeps breakage to a minimum. These are especially good when served with Cucumber-Dill Sauce alongside.

Rinse the flounder fillets and pat them dry.

In a wide shallow dish, whisk together the eggs and water and season with salt and pepper to taste.

Spread the flour on a large plate and season with salt and pepper to taste.

Spread the bread crumbs evenly on a large plate and season lightly with salt and pepper to taste.

Bread the fish fillets, one at a time, in the seasoned flour, and shake off the excess. Dip the fillet into the egg wash, and lastly dredge it in the bread crumbs, coating completely and patting the crumbs on if necessary. Arrange on a platter or baking sheet. Coat the remaining fillets in the same way. When all the fillets are breaded, cover them loosely with plastic wrap and put in the refrigerator until cooking time.

In a large skillet, heat ¼ inch oil until hot. Add enough of the chilled fillets to fit in the skillet without crowding, and fry them over medium-high heat until golden brown, 3 to 4 minutes, depending upon thickness. Turn

8 medium flounder fillets

4 extra-large eggs, beaten lightly

¼ cup water

Coarse kosher salt and fresh pepper, to taste

2 to 3 cups all-purpose flour

3 to 4 cups Homemade Bread Crumbs (page 62)

Flavorless vegetable oil, for sautéing

Cucumber-Dill Sauce (page 219), for serving

the fillets carefully with a spatula and fry until golden on the second side. Remove the fillets to paper towels to drain. Cook the remaining fillets in the same manner.

Serve hot, with the chilled Cucumber-Dill Sauce.

FRIED HALIBUT FINGERS

MAKES 8 SERVINGS, OF 2 PIECES EACH

These are crispy on the outside but wonderfully moist within, and should be served the minute they're ready. I knew I had a winner of a recipe when two of my grandsons, Teddy and Jeremy, eleven and eight years old, respectively, gave me the thumbs-up when they tasted them.

❖

Cut the halibut pieces into strips, each 4 inches long and about 1 inch wide.

In a shallow, wide dish, whisk the milk, egg, and water and season with salt and pepper to taste.

Spread the flour on a plate, and season with salt and pepper to taste.

Pour the bread crumbs onto a large plate, season with salt and pepper to taste, and spread in an even layer.

Dip the fish strips, one at a time, first into the flour, and shake off any excess. Dip the strip into the egg mixture, and lastly dredge it in the bread crumbs, coating strips completely. Place the strips as they are breaded in one layer on a large plate.

Heat 1 inch of vegetable oil in a wide skillet or sauté pan over high heat until hot. Add enough breaded strips to fit without crowding the pan and fry a total of 4 to 5 minutes, turning with a metal spatula about halfway through, until

4 pieces skinless halibut
   (6 ounces each, or
   1½ pounds total)
1 cup milk
1 extra-large egg, beaten lightly
½ cup water
Coarse kosher salt and fresh
   pepper, to taste
½ cup all-purpose flour, for
   dredging
1 to 1½ cups Homemade Bread
   Crumbs (page 62)
Flavorless vegetable oil, for
   frying

nicely browned and really crispy on the outside. Fry the remaining strips in the same manner. Serve at once, when they are at their crispiest.

VEGETABLES, SIDE DISHES, AND SALADS

VEGETABLES ◈ 129

Red Cabbage with Apples ◈ *Tzimmes* ◈ Parsleyed Potatoes ◈ *Kartoffelpuree* (Mashed Potatoes) ◈ *Krautfleckerl* (Cabbage, Caramelized Onions, and Bow-tie Pasta) ◈ Peas and Carrots with White Sauce ◈ Potato Dumplings ◈ Potato Pancakes ◈ Pepper Ragout ◈ Cauliflower with Toasted Crumbs ◈ *Variation:* Savoy Cabbage with Toasted Crumbs

SIDE DISHES ◈ 147

Risi Bisi (Rice and Peas) ◈ Lentil and Rice Pilaf ◈ Brown Rice with Mushrooms ◈ Kasha ◈ Barley Pilaf with Shiitake Mushrooms and Onion ◈ Bow-Ties with Toasted Crumbs ◈ Farina Dumplings

SALADS ◈ 159

Grüne Salat (Green Salad with Sweet Dressing) ◈ Cinnamon-Scented Salad ◈ Chopped Salad ◈ Green Salad with Ginger Dressing ◈ Romaine and Cucumber Salad with Radishes and Tomatoes ◈ Cucumber Salad ◈ Sliced Beet Salad ◈ Tomato, Red Onion, Cucumber, and Parsley Salad ◈ Endive and Red and Golden Beet Salad with Scallion Dressing ◈ Cole Slaw ◈ Green Bean and Red Onion Salad ◈ Pea Salad ◈ Potato Salad ◈ Light Potato Salad

VEGETABLES

Red Cabbage
with Apples

MAKES 6 TO 8 SERVINGS

1 head red cabbage (about
   2 pounds), cored and
   shredded
3 tablespoons sugar
2 teaspoons coarse kosher salt
½ cup white vinegar
2 medium McIntosh apples
1 medium onion
2 to 3 tablespoons flavorless
   vegetable oil
1 medium onion, peeled and
   studded with 10 whole cloves
1 bay leaf
2 cups boiling water

The cabbage and vinegar make it sour, the apples and sugar make it sweet, but by the time it has finished cooking, it is mellow in flavor, beyond comforting in texture. I serve it, untraditionally, with Brisket (page 69)—a delicious combination.

◆

Put the cabbage in a large glass or ceramic bowl, add the sugar, salt, and vinegar, and stir well to combine. Let stand at room temperature for 1 hour. Drain well.

Meanwhile, peel, core, and chop the apples. Chop the onion (you should have about 1 cup).

In a large skillet or sauté pan, heat the oil over medium heat until hot. Add the chopped apples and onion, and cook, stirring, until the onion pieces are translucent and the apples slightly golden, 6 to 8 minutes.

Stir in the drained cabbage, add the whole onion, bay leaf, and boiling water, and bring the mixture to a boil. Reduce the heat to low, cover the pan, and simmer, stirring occasionally, for 1½ hours to 2 hours, until the liquid has cooked almost completely off.

To serve, remove and discard the whole onion and bay leaf. Spoon the cabbage into a serving bowl and serve hot.

TZIMMES

MAKES 4 TO 6 SERVINGS

Apples, prunes, sweet potatoes, and brown sugar make this *tzimmes*, which is typically sweet, even sweeter and almost jamlike in texture. It is a wonderful accompaniment to Roast Turkey with Apple, Almond, and Raisin Stuffing (page 115), or on a simpler note, Roast Chicken with Bread Stuffing (page 101).

In a large saucepan, combine all the ingredients over medium heat. Bring to a gentle simmer, cover, and cook over medium-low heat, stirring occasionally, for 1½ hours, or until the mixture has thickened and is almost jamlike in texture. Transfer to a serving dish and serve hot.

4 cups peeled, chopped carrots (about 6 large)

1 cup peeled, cored, chopped McIntosh apple (2 medium)

2 cups chopped peeled sweet potato (1 large)

2½ cups pitted prunes

½ cup packed brown sugar

½ teaspoon ground nutmeg

¼ teaspoon ground cinnamon

5 cups water

PARSLEYED POTATOES

6 medium-large red potatoes,
    peeled
Coarse kosher salt, to taste
¼ cup chopped fresh parsley

With Oma, there was definitely a right way and a wrong way of doing things. And this applied to the peeling of potatoes. For some reason I could not do it, and eventually Oma stopped asking. Little wonder: Half the potato was going out with the peel! So Oma saw to the peeling and a good thing that was, too, because we had these delicious potatoes often. She liked to serve these alongside goulash or stew, two other dishes she loved.

I like to add these into Veal Stew with Tomatoes and Green Pepper (page 91). The stew lends them color and flavor, but, best of all, softens them slightly on the outsides. These potatoes remind me of how good the simplest of recipes can be.

Put the potatoes in a large saucepan, cover with cold water, and add salt to taste. Bring the water to a boil over medium-high heat. Reduce the heat to medium-low and boil gently for 15 to 20 minutes, until the potatoes can be easily pierced with a fork. Drain.

Transfer the potatoes to a serving bowl, sprinkle with the chopped parsley, and serve.

KARTOFFELPUREE

(Mashed Potatoes)

MAKES 6 SERVINGS

I make mashed potatoes with margarine and soy milk when I am serving them with meat. Use butter in place of the margarine, if you wish, and milk. Mashed Potatoes, it turns out, are quite a personal thing: smooth or lumpy? You decide.

Elisabeth Pozzi-Thanner shared with me her mother's collection of favorite recipes—all recopied by hand in a book for keepsaking—and mentioned that mashed potatoes are *the* side dish for *Fleischlabel* (page 76). Seasoned meat patties with mashed potatoes—what could be better? You might also try them with Meat Loaf (page 79), Meat Kabobs (page 78), or *Backhendl* (Fried Chicken, Viennese Style, page 107).

6 large russet potatoes, peeled

4 tablespoons (½ stick) unsalted margarine

Soy milk as needed

Coarse kosher salt and fresh pepper, to taste

Cut the potatoes into quarters and put them in a large saucepan. Cover with cold water, and bring to a boil over medium-high heat. Boil the potatoes for 15 to 20 minutes, or until tender when pierced with a fork. Drain, and return the potatoes to the saucepan.

With a potato masher, break the potatoes into pieces, add the margarine, and continue mashing, adding soy milk to reach the desired consistency. (I like mashed potatoes with a little texture, as opposed to smooth and silky.

The finished product is entirely up to you.) Season with salt and pepper to taste, and either serve immediately, or transfer to the top of a double boiler and hold over hot water for 30 minutes.

KRAUTFLECKERL

(Cabbage, Caramelized Onions, and Bow-Tie Pasta)

MAKES 6 TO 8 SERVINGS

Oma was a woman of few words, and she was stern, but you knew immediately when she enjoyed something, and she loved this dish. *Kraut* means cabbage in German, and *fleckerl* means squares of dough. Oma made this with egg noodles. I've taken the liberty of using bow-ties, *farfalle* in Italian, instead of noodles or dough squares, which reflects my long-standing fondness for all things Italian.

This has an almost melt-in-your-mouth texture. I suspect Oma liked it for that reason, but even more for its Austrian-ness. It is one of my favorite dishes, too, especially when it accompanies stew or goulash.

Cut each cabbage quarter into long thin slices. Now cut the slices crosswise into thin pieces, about ½ inch in width. Set aside.

In a medium skillet, dissolve the sugar in the oil over medium-low heat, stirring, being careful not to splash the hot oil. Add the onion and cook, stirring occasionally, until well browned but not burnt, 6 to 8 minutes. Do not hurry this step. Stir in the paprika, add salt and pepper to taste, and cook, stirring, until the onion is completely coated with the paprika and colored a rich brown, several minutes. Remove the pan from the heat and set aside.

1 small green cabbage (1½ to 2 pounds), quartered and cored

1 teaspoon sugar

3 tablespoons flavorless vegetable oil

1 large onion, sliced

1 tablespoon sweet Hungarian paprika

Coarse kosher salt and fresh pepper, to taste

3 tablespoons water

2 cups bow-tie pasta, cooked according to the directions on the box, drained well, and reserved in a single layer on paper towels to air-dry at room temperature

In a large skillet, combine the cabbage and water. Cook over medium-high heat, stirring frequently, for about 20 minutes, until the cabbage is softened and browned.

When the cabbage is nicely colored and well cooked, add the caramelized onion and bow-ties to the skillet. Stir well to combine and cook over medium heat until the pasta and onion are reheated and the components are combined. Season with salt and pepper to taste, transfer to a serving bowl, and serve hot.

PEAS AND CARROTS WITH WHITE SAUCE

MAKES 6 TO 8 SERVINGS

With a little sautéed onion and garlic added for flavor and a light white sauce for texture, you can transform everyday peas and carrots into something unbelievably delicious. A smooth sauce is key and that means you need to whisk, and keep on whisking, as the sauce thickens.

Make this during the week, or for a special occasion, with Roast Turkey with Apple, Almond, and Raisin Stuffing (page 115), for example.

❖

Put the cooked peas and carrots in a large bowl.

In a small skillet, heat 1 tablespoon of the oil over medium heat until hot. Add the onion and cook, stirring, until softened and translucent, about 3 minutes. Add the garlic and cook, stirring, just until fragrant, about 30 seconds. Scrape the mixture into the bowl of vegetables and stir to combine.

In a 10-inch sauté pan, heat the remaining 3 tablespoons oil over medium heat. Add a pinch of sugar and the flour and cook, whisking constantly, until the flour turns lightly golden, 1 to 2 minutes. Begin adding the broth, a little at a time, whisking constantly. Continue to add broth, whisking constantly, until the sauce thickens. Reduce the heat to medium-low, and whisk over low heat until smooth, several minutes.

A total of 5½ cups combined cooked peas and carrot cubes
4 tablespoons flavorless vegetable oil
½ onion, finely chopped
1 large garlic clove, finely chopped
Pinch sugar
¼ cup all-purpose flour
2 cups chicken broth

Stir the vegetable mixture into the sauce, and cook over low heat long enough for the sauce to coat the vegetables, about 3 minutes. Stir gently; do not let the sauce boil. Remove the pan from the heat, transfer the vegetables to a bowl, and serve at once.

Potato Dumplings

MAKES 14 TO 16

Add these to stews, Shell Steak with Onions (page 95), in particular, or even to soups. You can also dust the dumplings with Toasted Crumbs (page 63), or sugared toasted crumbs, the ones used to finish Apricot Dumplings, for even more of a treat. These dumplings are delicate, light, and pretty, flecked as they are with a bit of chopped parsley. Key to their success is to boil the potatoes until tender to the touch—no longer.

❖

4 large Idaho potatoes, peeled
½ cup all-purpose flour, plus additional for your hands
1 teaspoon table salt
¼ cup Homemade Bread Crumbs (page 62)
1 extra-large egg, beaten lightly
2 teaspoons soy milk
1 tablespoon finely chopped fresh parsley

Place the potatoes in a medium-large saucepan and cover with cold water. Bring the water to a boil over medium-high heat and boil the potatoes gently for at least 15 minutes, until they are tender when tested with a fork. Do not overcook. Drain and let cool.

Rice the potatoes into a bowl (you should have about 3½ cups).

Bring a large pot of salted water to a boil over medium-high heat.

Add the flour, 1 teaspoon salt, bread crumbs, egg, soy milk, and parsley to the potatoes and stir with a wooden spoon or with your hands to form a smooth paste. Flour your hands lightly and shape the potato mixture into round dumplings, each about 1 inch in diameter; or use 2 tablespoons to shape the mixture into ovals, 1½ to 2 inches long. (You should have 14 to 16.)

When the water is boiling, add the dumplings, in batches. Bring the water back to a boil, then boil gently for 10 to 15 minutes. The dumplings will rise to the surface when they are done. With a slotted spoon, remove to a plate. Cook the remaining dumplings in the same manner.

Chill the dumplings in the refrigerator until cool, then add to stews or soups, as desired.

POTATO PANCAKES

MAKES ABOUT 2 DOZEN HALF-DOLLAR-SIZED PANCAKES

As anyone who has ever made latkes on Chanukah knows, they cannot be made in advance, and the sooner you serve them, the better they are. These are especially addictive, even without applesauce or sour cream, which are the customary accompaniments.

For a Chanukah dinner menu, including latkes, of course, see page 243.

❖

Line a baking sheet with paper towels.

Grate the potatoes, onions, carrots, and zucchini on the large holes of a box grater. Combine the grated vegetables in a large bowl, add the garlic, flour, and egg, and stir to combine well. Season well with salt and pepper to taste.

In a skillet or frying pan, heat ½ inch of vegetable oil over high heat until hot but not smoking. (If you have a deep-fat thermometer, it should register about 325 degrees F.)

While the oil is heating, make the pancakes: Shape enough batter to fill the palm of your hand into pancakes the size of silver dollars, pressing the batter together firmly. When the oil is hot enough for frying, add 6 to 8 pancakes at a time. Fry for 2 to 3 minutes on the first side, until golden brown. Turn and fry for an additional 2 to 3 minutes, until

2 pounds russet potatoes, peeled
2 medium onions
2 medium carrots, peeled
2 medium zucchini, trimmed
5 garlic cloves, minced
1 cup all-purpose flour
1 extra-large egg, beaten lightly
Coarse kosher salt and fresh pepper, to taste
Flavorless vegetable oil, for frying
Applesauce (page 220), sour cream, or both, for serving

golden brown all over. Remove with a slotted spoon to the towel-lined baking sheet to drain. Fry and drain the remaining pancakes in the same manner.

Serve as soon as possible, piping hot, with applesauce or sour cream.

PEPPER RAGOUT

MAKES 6 SERVINGS

I love this ragout just as is. I also use it as the base for a stew with chicken sausage (page 113), which is also delicious, and a more substantial, way to serve this.

The addition of potatoes is optional; if you serve this as a side dish with another starch, two starches may be too many. On the other hand, if you are making it to accompany a simple entrée, like Meat Kabobs (page 78), you probably will want the potatoes. I would, but you decide.

In a large saucepan, heat the olive oil over medium heat until hot. Add the garlic, and cook, stirring, until softened, about 10 minutes. Be careful not to let it burn.

Add the red and yellow peppers, tomatoes, red onion, and potatoes, if using, and stir to combine. Cover the pot, and cook, stirring occasionally, for 30 to 40 minutes, until the vegetables have softened almost to a stew.

Serve hot, or at room temperature. The ragout keeps in a covered container in the refrigerator for 5 days. Reheat over low heat to prevent scorching.

4 tablespoons extra-virgin olive oil

2 garlic cloves, chopped

3 large red bell peppers, cored, seeded, and sliced into thin strips

3 large yellow peppers, cored, seeded, and cut into thin strips

3 medium tomatoes, peeled and cut into chunks

1 medium red onion, sliced

4 Yukon gold potatoes, peeled and quartered, optional

Coarse kosher salt and fresh pepper, to taste

CAULIFLOWER WITH TOASTED CRUMBS

MAKES 6 SERVINGS

One 2½- to 3-pound head of cauliflower, leaves removed, cored, and cut into florets

1 cup Toasted Homemade Bread Crumbs (page 63), still in the pan and still hot from toasting

I can't describe how delicious everyday cauliflower becomes when you combine it with hot toasted, crunchy crumbs. Unlike other preparations, where crumbs serve as a garnish, the crumbs here are an ingredient, an important component, and as such you add the cooked florets to them, not the other way around, right before serving.

Serve this with My Mother's Chicken Paprika (page 103), Fried Chicken, Viennese Style (page 107), or Meat Kabobs (page 78), and that is just a start.

❖

Bring a large pot of water to a boil over high heat, add the cauliflower, and boil gently for 10 to 15 minutes, or until tender when pierced with a fork. Drain in a colander.

Add the drained florets to the skillet of hot crumbs, and toss gently to combine.

Transfer the crumbed florets to a serving bowl, and serve at once, while the crumbs are still hot and toasty.

Variation

SAVOY CABBAGE WITH TOASTED CRUMBS

This combination for Savoy cabbage with crumbs was given to me by my oldest daughter, Laura, who learned it from her great-aunt, Ciel, my mother's sister. Including Laura's children, this recipe has now been handed down to four generations.

Halve a 1½-pound Savoy cabbage, remove the core, and cut each half crosswise into ½-inch slices, then cut the slices crosswise into ¾-inch pieces. (You should have between 5 and 6 cups chopped cabbage.) Bring a large pot of salted water to a boil over high heat, add the cabbage, and boil 6 to 8 minutes, or until tender. Drain well in a colander.

Have ready 1 cup Toasted Homemade Bread Crumbs (page 63). Add the drained hot cabbage to the skillet of hot crumbs and toss gently to combine.

Transfer the crumbed cabbage to a serving bowl and serve at once.

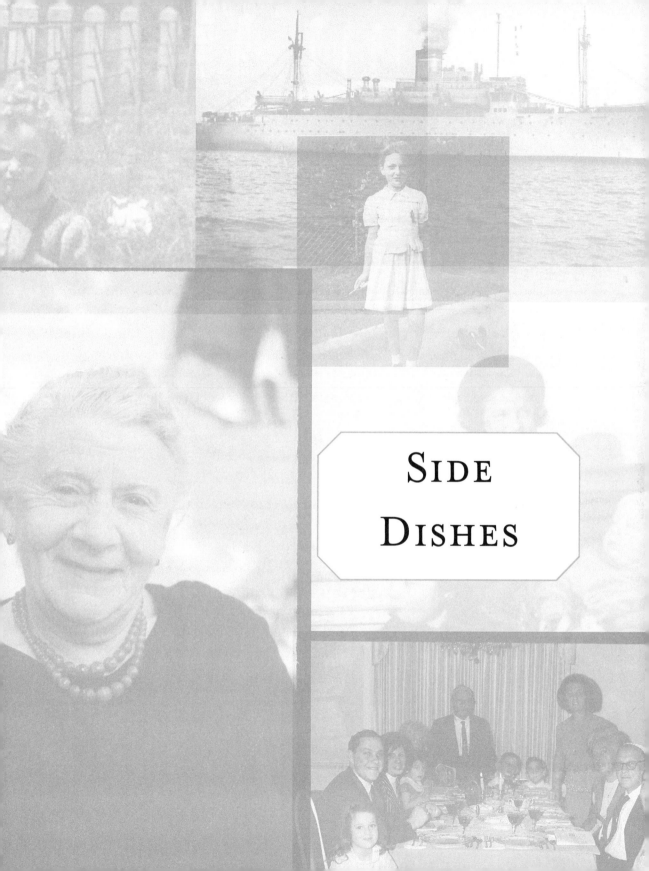

SIDE
DISHES

RISI BISI

(Rice and Peas)

MAKES 8 SERVINGS

4 cups water

2 cups long-grain rice

4 tablespoons (½ stick) unsalted margarine, in pieces

1 tablespoon salt

1 bay leaf

2 cups frozen garden peas, cooked, drained, and still hot

The very mention of Italy, where I spent the first five years of my life, makes me happy, which is why I call this favorite dish of mine, white rice with green peas, by its Italian name. I like to serve this with another dish from my childhood, My Mother's Chicken Paprika (page 103). *Risi Bisi* is also the traditional accompaniment to *Backhendl* (Fried Chicken, Viennese Style, page 107). It is wonderful with many dishes, and it will always be close to my heart.

Preheat the oven to 350 degrees F.

In a flameproof 2½-quart casserole, bring the water to a boil over high heat. Stir in the rice, then add the margarine, salt, and bay leaf and cook until the margarine melts and the water comes to a boil. Cover and transfer the casserole to the oven.

Bake for 20 minutes, until all the water is absorbed.

Remove the bay leaf. Fluff the rice with a fork, add the peas, and toss gently to incorporate.

LENTIL AND RICE PILAF

MAKES 6 TO 8 SERVINGS

You start this recipe on the stovetop, then transfer it to the oven, which insures even cooking every time. The combination of lentils and rice is a tried-and-true one, is a little different, and goes well with almost any grilled, sautéed, or roasted meat or fish.

Preheat the oven to 350 degrees.

In a flameproof 2½-quart casserole, heat the oil over medium-high heat until hot. Add the onion, reduce the heat to medium, and cook, stirring, until lightly golden, 6 to 10 minutes. Add the lentils and cook, stirring, for 5 minutes. Stir in the salt and water and bring to a boil. Add the bay leaf and rice, and bring the mixture to a boil. Cover and transfer the casserole to the oven.

Bake for 25 to 30 minutes, until all the water is absorbed and the rice is tender.

Before serving, remove the bay leaf and fluff the pilaf with a fork.

3 tablespoons flavorless vegetable oil
1 medium yellow onion, thinly sliced
1 cup lentils, picked over
½ tablespoon coarse kosher salt
4 cups boiling water
1 bay leaf
2 cups long-grain white rice

Brown Rice with Mushrooms

MAKES 6 SERVINGS

1 tablespoon unsalted butter

1 tablespoon flavorless
vegetable oil

1 small onion, sliced (1 cup)

2 cups sliced mushrooms

1 cup brown rice

2½ cups water

1 bay leaf

1 small fresh thyme sprig

Boiled on the stovetop, brown rice can be challenging to cook evenly. Bake it in the oven, as I do here, and it turns out perfectly every time.

With the mushrooms, this brown rice is elegant enough to accompany veal stew. I often pair it with Pepper Ragout (see page 143).

Preheat the oven to 350 degrees F.

In a flameproof 2½-quart casserole, heat the butter and oil over medium-high heat until the butter is no longer foamy. Add the onion and mushrooms and cook, stirring, until the onion is translucent and the mushrooms are soft, about 10 minutes.

Add the rice, and cook, stirring, until completely coated, about 2 minutes. Add the water, bay leaf, and thyme, and bring the water to a boil. Cover and transfer the casserole to the oven.

Bake for 35 minutes, until all the water is absorbed.

Before serving, remove the bay leaf and thyme sprig and fluff the rice with a fork.

KASHA

Buckwheat Groats

MAKES 4 SERVINGS

Oma's favorite starch was potatoes, her boiled potatoes (page 132). I'm not sure if she ever even tasted kasha. Along with brown rice, it has become one of my favorite side dishes. It is different, relatively quick to prepare, and good with both meat and chicken.

When you cook the kasha with the egg, stir continually, otherwise the egg will scramble.

❖

4 cups chicken broth

2 cups kasha

1 extra-large egg, beaten lightly

3 tablespoons flavorless
    vegetable oil

1 small onion, chopped

2 cups sliced mushrooms

Coarse kosher salt and fresh
    pepper, to taste

In a large saucepan, bring the chicken broth to a boil over medium heat.

Meanwhile, pour the kasha into a medium sauté pan or skillet. Add the beaten egg, and cook over medium-low, stirring constantly, until each kernel of kasha is separate and coated with egg. When the broth is at a boil, stir the kasha mixture into the broth. Reduce the heat, cover the saucepan, and simmer gently until the broth is completely absorbed, 10 to 15 minutes. Remove from the heat and keep covered.

In medium skillet, heat the oil over medium heat until hot. Add the onion, and cook, stirring, until translucent, about 3 minutes. Stir in the mushrooms and cook, stirring, until softened and the liquid has cooked off, 8 to

10 minutes. Season with salt and pepper to taste, then stir the mushroom mixture into the cooked kasha. Taste, adjust the seasonings and serve.

Barley Pilaf with Shiitake Mushrooms and Onion

MAKES 6 TO 8 SERVINGS

Barley makes this pilaf unique, and the shiitake mushrooms make it stylish enough for a holiday meal. Unlike dried beans, barley does not require overnight soaking, which makes this a doable weeknight side dish, too.

Put the barley in a saucepan and add 4 cups water and 1 teaspoon salt. Bring the water to a boil, lower the heat to medium, and simmer the barley for about 25 minutes, or until softened. Drain and keep warm, covered.

While the barley is cooking, heat the oil in a large skillet until hot over medium-high heat. Add the mushrooms and onion, and sauté, stirring, until the mushrooms are softened and the onion is golden, about 10 minutes. Season with salt and pepper to taste.

Stir the hot barley into the mushroom mixture and combine. Adjust the seasonings. Transfer the pilaf to a serving bowl.

2 cups pearl barley, rinsed in water and drained

4 cups water

1 teaspoon coarse kosher salt, plus additional to taste

2 tablespoons flavorless vegetable oil

2 cups sliced shiitake mushrooms

1 small onion, diced (about 1 cup)

Fresh pepper, to taste

BOW-TIES WITH TOASTED CRUMBS

MAKES 8 SERVINGS

8 ounces (½ pound) bow-tie pasta, cooked according to the directions on the box and well drained

1 cup Toasted Homemade Bread Crumbs (page 63)

Oma liked to toss wide egg noodles with toasted crumbs, then serve them alongside stew or goulash. Here I've simply substituted *farfalle*, bow-ties, for the egg noodles. And like Oma, I serve these with stew, too—Veal Stew with Mushrooms (page 93), in particular.

Double the amount of pasta if you are serving a crowd, but double and then some the crumbs. You can't have enough of the toasty crumbs, in my opinion.

❖

Reheat the bow-ties, if necessary, in a saucepan of boiling water until hot. Drain well.

Transfer the bow-ties to a serving bowl, add the toasted crumbs, and toss gently. Serve while the crumbs are still hot and crunchy.

A FORMATIVE FIRST IMPRESSION

My love for Italian food began when my family lived in Italy as "free prisoners" for the first five years of my life. The warm, sun-filled country that was our safe haven will always hold a special place in my heart—as will its delicious, unpretentious food.

My father had a singsong saying about our simple, wonderful meals in Italy. He repeated it often, and I loved it: "*Montag, pasta; Dienstag, pasta, Mittwoch, wieder pasta; Donnerstag, pasta, Freitag, pasta, Samstag, pasta, Sonntag, pasta.*" ("Monday, pasta; Tuesday, pasta; Wednesday, again pasta; Thursday, pasta; Friday, pasta; Saturday, pasta; Sunday, pasta.")

Pasta, pasta, and more pasta! He loved it; we all loved it. My mother, it turned out, after eating pasta for five years straight, had another response: "If I ever eat pasta again," she said, "it will be too soon!"

Not me. I still love it.

When I was about seven years old and living in the Bronx, my mother and Aunt Ciel took me out to dinner at a local Italian restaurant. Italian food, I could hardly wait! The pasta arrived, I took a big bite, then said to myself, "Not the pasta I remember."

Even then, I knew that the food in Italy was special.

Farina Dumplings

3 cups water

2½ teaspoons coarse kosher
  salt

3 tablespoons unsalted
  margarine

1½ cups regular farina

3 extra-large eggs

3 tablespoons finely chopped
  fresh parsley

Flour, for dredging

These dumplings are simple and filling. They satisfy in a quiet kind of way; I think of them as comfort food. Add them to Beef Broth (page 47), or to chicken soup in place of matzo balls.

Look for farina in the cereal aisle of the supermarket. Do not buy the instant variety for this recipe.

In a 2- to 3-quart saucepan, bring the water, salt, and margarine to a boil over medium-high heat. Slowly pour the farina into the boiling water, stirring constantly with a spoon as you pour. Reduce the heat to a simmer, and cook, continuing to stir, until the farina thickens enough to hold its shape on the spoon. Remove the pan from the heat.

Beat the eggs, one at a time, into the farina, stirring well to incorporate. Stir in the parsley. Let the mixture cool slightly, then shape the mixture into oval-shaped dumplings using 2 large soup spoons: Scoop a spoonful of the farina mixture up with one spoon and transfer it back and forth to the second spoon to shape and firm it into an oval. Transfer to a plate. Repeat with the remaining farina mixture. (You should have 24 oval dumplings, each about 2 inches long.)

Meanwhile, bring 2 quarts salted water to a boil over high heat in a large soup pot.

Spread enough flour to coat the dumplings out on a plate and roll the dumplings, one at a time, until coated.

When the water is at a rolling boil, add half the dumplings (they will sink to the bottom of the pot). Boil until they rise to the surface, about 5 minutes. Remove with a slotted spoon to a plate. Cook the remaining dumplings in the same manner.

To serve, add the dumplings to soup, let them heat through, then serve. To store, let cool and transfer to freezer bags. Freeze individually, or two to a bag, or in larger quantities for up to 3 months. To serve, add the frozen dumplings to your soup pot and heat over gentle heat for about 20 minutes, or until thawed.

SALADS

GRÜNE SALAT

(Green Salad with Sweet Dressing)

MAKES 6 TO 8 SERVINGS

1 medium-to-large head Boston lettuce, leaves removed whole, rinsed, and patted dry

FOR THE SWEET DRESSING
½ cup orange juice
6 tablespoons flavorless vegetable oil
2 tablespoons red wine vinegar
1 teaspoon honey
Coarse kosher salt and fresh pepper, to taste

*G*rüne salat, green salad—that is what Oma called it, which makes it sound plain. It wasn't. The dressing was sweet, which I've come to learn is the Austrian tradition (salads were sometimes served with just a dusting of sugar for dressing).

This was Oma's everyday salad. It was never served as a separate course. This is very close to her version: It was delicious then, and still is.

❖

Put the lettuce in a large salad bowl.

Make the dressing: In a small bowl, whisk together all the dressing ingredients until well combined and the honey is incorporated.

Pour the dressing over the salad, toss gently with tongs or your hands, and serve.

SIMPLE IS BEST

There was nothing extravagant about the food my grandmother made. It was straightforward fare. Oma was a responsible, serious woman and as head of the household, kept to a careful budget. Servings reflected that. Amounts were portioned out carefully. And you ate what was on your plate. Neither my sister nor myself would have ever dreamed of saying, "But I don't like that."

I wasn't aware of it at the time, but I realize now the impression Oma's way of doing things made on me over the years. It can be seen in her *grüne salat*. Simple is best. You don't need fancy ingredients. Take the green salads in this book. They are different in the details—how the ingredients are cut, or the use of vinegar, or lemon juice, or the oil.

Most of all, the ingredients are fresh. Oma went shopping just about every day.

Cinnamon-Scented Salad

MAKES 6 TO 8 SERVINGS WITH OTHER FIRST COURSES

1 medium head Boston lettuce, rinsed and leaves patted dry

1 medium head green leaf lettuce, rinsed, leaves patted dry and torn into pieces

3 tablespoons olive oil

1 tablespoon white wine vinegar

1 tablespoon sugar

Pinch ground cinnamon

Granulated sugar has been used to "dress" lettuce, so why not a touch of cinnamon? Its aroma is fleeting. You almost don't know it's there; you sense it for an instant, and then it is gone—a touch of sweet mystery.

Combine the Boston lettuce and green leaf lettuce in a large salad bowl. Toss to combine.

Shortly before serving, add the oil, vinegar, and sugar. Toss with tongs or your hands until the leaves are completely coated. Dust with cinnamon, toss very lightly, and serve, before the aroma disappears.

CHOPPED SALAD

Chop each vegetable the old-fashioned way—by hand. Chop fine, but do not mince. And be sure to use iceberg lettuce: You want its unique crispness and crunch. Then allow enough time for the salad to chill and the flavors to blend.

Cut the lettuce into thin wedges, then cut the wedges crosswise into small pieces. Rinse the chopped lettuce in a large bowl of cold water and drain well in a colander. Transfer the lettuce to a salad spinner and spin as dry as possible. Remove the lettuce to a double layer of paper towels and blot dry. Wrap the lettuce in a clean kitchen towel and refrigerate briefly to crisp.

While the lettuce crisps, chop the cucumbers, tomatoes, and onion into small pieces, similar in size to the pieces of lettuce. Place each as it is done in a glass serving bowl. Add the chilled lettuce. Drizzle the oil and lemon juice over the salad and toss well to combine. Cover the bowl with plastic wrap and refrigerate until just chilled.

Right before serving, sprinkle the salad with salt to taste, toss again, and serve at once, while still chilled.

½ large head iceberg lettuce, cored

2 large cucumbers, peeled and seeded

3 ripe tomatoes, cored

½ large white onion

3 tablespoons flavorless vegetable oil

1 tablespoon fresh lemon juice

Coarse kosher salt, to taste

GREEN SALAD WITH GINGER DRESSING

SERVES 6 TO 8

1 head Bibb lettuce, rinsed, leaves patted dry and torn into pieces

1 medium head romaine lettuce, rinsed, leaves patted dry and torn into pieces

4 scallions, ends trimmed, chopped into ¼-inch pieces

FOR THE GINGER DRESSING

⅓ cup flavorless vegetable oil

¼ cup white wine vinegar

2 tablespoons sugar

2 teaspoons soy sauce

½ teaspoon ground ginger

½ teaspoon fresh pepper

¼ teaspoon coarse kosher salt

I served this one Friday night dinner at a family gathering as a first course with challah, and there was not one lettuce leaf left in the bowl. The combination is easy to make and, judging from my own family's response, easy to like.

❖

In a large salad bowl, toss the Bibb lettuce with the romaine and scallions until combined.

Make the ginger dressing: In a medium bowl, whisk together all the dressing ingredients.

Pour the dressing over the salad, toss, and serve.

Romaine and Cucumber Salad with Radishes and Tomatoes

MAKES 6 TO 8 SERVINGS AS A FIRST COURSE

When I served this at one of my tasting dinners, two friends, both very knowledgeable about food, had seconds, and another, a wonderful cook, had thirds. And that was only the first course!

Add a little extra oil or lemon juice, if you like. And serve with black bread.

❖

Combine all the salad ingredients on a wide shallow platter. Toss gently to combine.

Add the oil and lemon juice and salt and pepper to taste and toss again.

2 large cucumbers, peeled and sliced ¼ inch thick

1 medium head romaine lettuce, rinsed, leaves patted dry and torn into pieces

1 cup whole radishes, rinsed well, ends trimmed, and thinly sliced

3 medium tomatoes, cored and cut into ½-inch cubes

¼ cup chopped fresh dill

½ cup minced fresh parsley

1 garlic clove, minced

3 tablespoons flavorless vegetable oil

1 tablespoon fresh lemon juice

Coarse kosher salt and fresh pepper, to taste

CUCUMBER SALAD

5 or 6 medium cucumbers,
   peeled and sliced paper-thin
   (about 9 cups sliced)
¾ tablespoon coarse kosher salt
¾ cup white vinegar
½ cup water
2 tablespoons sugar
½ medium onion, thinly sliced

This salad gets better and better tasting as it stands. I love it the first day, and the second day, too. There is no third day; it's gone by then. You want to slice the cucumbers as thin as possible, literally see-through, if you can. A mandoline does the job perfectly (so will a sharp knife and a steady hand).

If you are wondering where the oil in the dressing is, there isn't any. I don't make it with oil. If you like oil in salad, add it, but only a little.

This salad pairs exquisitely with Sliced Beet Salad (page 167). There is nothing like the combination of colors, flavor, and texture.

❖

Put the cucumber slices in a large colander, sprinkle with the salt, and toss to combine. Place the colander over a bowl and let the cucumbers drain for about 1 hour. (Quite a bit of liquid will drain off.) Transfer the slices to a large serving bowl.

In a small bowl, whisk together the vinegar, water, and sugar until the sugar is dissolved.

Pour the dressing over the cucumbers and stir well. Add the onion and stir to combine. Cover the bowl with plastic wrap and refrigerate until ready to serve. Serve well chilled.

Sliced Beet Salad

This salad is testimony to just how good beets can be. If you have made my Cucumber Salad (page 166), you already know that I like to serve it and this salad at the same time. At the risk of repeating myself, they are meant for each other.

Bring a large pot of water to a boil over medium-high heat, add the beets, and simmer until fork-tender, 30 to 40 minutes depending on the size. Drain, let cool, peel, and cut into thin slices. Put the slices in a glass serving bowl.

Add the remaining ingredients to the beets, and toss gently to combine. Cover with plastic wrap, and chill.

Toss the salad again just before serving.

1½ pounds red beets, trimmed of greens and washed (about 5 medium-large)

1 cup thinly sliced white onion (1 large)

½ cup red wine vinegar

⅓ cup flavorless vegetable oil

1 tablespoon sugar

1 teaspoon drained prepared horseradish

¼ teaspoon coarse kosher salt

Tomato, Red Onion, Cucumber, and Parsley Salad

MAKES 6 GENEROUS SERVINGS

4 medium tomatoes, cored

2 medium cucumbers, peeled

1 medium red onion

3 tablespoons chopped fresh parsley

3 tablespoons flavorless vegetable oil

1 tablespoon fresh lemon juice

Coarse kosher salt and fresh pepper, to taste

If you substitute an ingredient or two below, and chop them fine—as opposed to cubing them as you do for this salad—you make another of my favorites, Chopped Salad on page 163. Similar but different, and both are superb.

For a most wonderful summer lunch, serve this with Deviled Eggs (page 32) and Liptauer (page 29) with black bread, sweet butter, sliced radishes, chopped scallions, and minced chives.

Cube the tomatoes, cucumbers, and red onion by hand into pieces ½ inch in size. Combine them in a large salad bowl. Add the chopped parsley, oil, and lemon juice and toss well, with tongs or your hands, to combine.

Just before serving, season with salt and pepper to taste, toss again, and serve.

Endive and Red and Golden Beet Salad with Scallion Dressing

MAKES 8 GENEROUS SERVINGS

Two different-colored beets, pale-green endive spears, and a vivid green dressing make this one of the most beautiful—and most delicious—salads I have ever tasted.

❖

Cook the beets: Cook the beets in separate saucepans: Bring 2 large pans with enough water to cover the beets to a boil over medium-high heat. Add the golden beets to one pan and the red beets to the other. Simmer 30 to 40 minutes, or until fork-tender. Drain, let cool, and peel. (Do not combine the beets or the red beet juice will color the golden beets.) Cut the golden beets into thin slices and put in a medium bowl. Cut the red beets into similar slices and put in another bowl. Divide the oil and vinegar evenly between them. Toss and let the beets stand at room temperature to develop flavor while you prepare the dressing.

Make the scallion dressing: In a blender or food processor fitted with the metal blade, combine all the ingredients, except the oil, and blend until almost smooth. With the machine running, add the oil in a slow, steady stream, and process until totally combined. Taste and adjust the seasonings, if desired.

FOR THE BEETS

3 medium golden beets, trimmed of greens

3 medium red beets, trimmed of greens

3 tablespoons flavorless vegetable oil

1 tablespoon red wine vinegar

FOR THE SCALLION DRESSING

4 scallions, trimmed and coarsely chopped

4 garlic cloves, coarsely chopped

1 tablespoon water

1 tablespoon sugar

½ tablespoon Dijon mustard

¾ teaspoon coarse kosher salt

¼ teaspoon fresh pepper

2 cups flavorless vegetable oil

4 large or 6 small heads of endive

Assemble the salad: Cut the stem ends off the endive, and remove the leaves one by one. Arrange the leaves, fanning them out from the center, on a wide, shallow serving platter with sides. Spoon the sliced red and golden beets decoratively in the center of the leaves and drizzle with some of the scallion dressing. Pour the remaining dressing into a server and pass it with the salad at the table.

Cole Slaw

My youngest daughter, Dena, has always loved this very simple recipe of mine for cole slaw. She has perfected it by providing precise measurements to maximize the flavor. Prepare it ahead of time, cover it, and let it marinate in the refrigerator. The longer it stands the better.

Put the cabbage and onion in a large salad bowl and toss to combine.

In a small ceramic bowl, stir the lemon juice into the sugar to form a paste.

Scrape the sugar mixture over the cabbage and onion and stir it in well. Add the mayonnaise and stir until thoroughly incorporated. Cover the bowl with plastic wrap, and refrigerate for at least several hours, preferably overnight, to allow the flavors to blend.

1½ to 2 pounds green cabbage, cored and shredded

1 small onion, grated on the small holes of a hand-held box grater

½ cup fresh lemon juice (3 or 4 lemons)

1 cup sugar

1 cup mayonnaise

Green Bean and Red Onion Salad

MAKES 6 SERVINGS

1 pound green beans, tips
    removed

1 small red onion, thinly sliced

½ teaspoon coarse kosher salt

3 tablespoons flavorless
    vegetable oil

1 tablespoon red wine vinegar

1 tablespoon chopped fresh
    parsley

1 tablespoon chopped fresh dill

Fresh pepper, to taste

This is my version of Oma's *Bohnensalat,* green bean salad. The addition of fresh herbs is mine. I love green beans cooked until they are a little soft; others like them crisp. It is up to you as to how long to cook them.

This is pretty in its own simple way and goes well with heavier dishes, like Brisket (page 69) or goulash. The salad will taste best if you make it slightly ahead of time, which allows the flavors, especially the red onion, to develop.

Bring a medium saucepan of salted water to a boil over medium heat. Add the beans and boil them gently until they are cooked to your taste. Drain and immediately run under cold water until cool. Pat the beans dry with paper towels.

In a serving bowl, combine the beans with all the remaining ingredients, and toss. Cover loosely with plastic wrap and let stand at room temperature for 30 minutes. Or, cover tightly and chill if serving at a later time.

Taste, and adjust the seasonings before serving.

PEA SALAD

My daughter Laura shared this recipe with me, and when I served this salad at one of my tasting dinners, my cousin Ruth, who is a wonderful cook, wanted to know what the "seasoning" was. I said, "A touch of sugar?" to which Ruth replied, "No, it's something else." Seeing how there are so few ingredients, I said, "The vinegar?" Ruth shook her head, suspecting, I think, a special ingredient. There are no special, or complicated, ingredients in this. It reminds me of an "Oma" salad—a lovely combination that is sweet and simple and green—even without lettuce— easy to make, and, apparently, intriguing. I still don't know what seasoning Ruth thought she tasted.

1 (16 ounce) bag frozen peas, thawed and drained
½ cup thinly sliced celery
1 cup thinly sliced scallions, green and white parts
¼ to ½ cup chopped green bell pepper
1 teaspoon sugar
½ teaspoon coarse kosher salt
Fresh pepper, to taste
¼ cup mayonnaise
1 teaspoon white vinegar

In a salad bowl, gently combine the peas, celery, scallions, and green pepper. Sprinkle the sugar, salt, and pepper to taste over the vegetables and toss. Add the mayonnaise and vinegar and toss to combine well. Cover the salad with plastic wrap, and chill about 1 hour.

Before serving, taste and adjust the seasonings, if desired.

POTATO SALAD

MAKES 4 TO 6 SERVINGS AS A SIDE DISH

2 pounds red potatoes, boiled in skins until fork-tender, drained, cooled, then sliced thick

1½ teaspoons salt

2 scallions, chopped

½ cup chopped red bell pepper

½ cup chopped green bell pepper

½ cup mayonnaise

Fresh pepper, to taste

When you have five healthy and growing children to feed, as we did, it is almost impossible to have too much food. The bigger they got, the more food I needed. Salads like this one were always a hit, and they could easily be doubled or tripled—a good thing, because there was always an extra friend, or two, or three, over for dinner when we lived in King's Point.

Make this ahead of time, cover, and refrigerate. It will only improve in flavor.

In a bowl, gently fold all the ingredients together with a large spoon or plastic spatula until combined. Adjust the seasonings to taste, cover with plastic wrap, and refrigerate until lightly chilled, about 1 hour.

LIGHT POTATO SALAD

MAKES 6 SERVINGS

This recipe, with its handful of ingredients—vinaigrette, scallions, and potatoes—*is* light in comparison to so many other potato salad extravaganzas. In fact, its simplicity and integrity of flavor, are, in large part, its appeal. Dress it while the potatoes are still warm for the vinaigrette to have maximum impact.

With Fried Flounder (page 123) and a green salad or beet salad, this makes a wonderful summer supper.

◈

10 small new potatoes, scrubbed but not peeled
2 scallions, ends trimmed and both white and green parts chopped
3 tablespoons flavorless vegetable oil
1 tablespoon white vinegar
Coarse kosher salt and fresh pepper

Put the potatoes in a large saucepan, cover with cold water, and bring the water to a boil over medium-high heat. Simmer gently until the potatoes are just tender when pierced with the tip of a knife. Drain and let cool just long enough to handle. Halve (or quarter) the potatoes and put in a serving bowl. Add the scallions.

In a small bowl, whisk together the oil and vinegar, pour the mixture over the still-warm potatoes, and toss gently to dress. Season with salt and pepper to taste.

Let the salad stand at room temperature to develop flavor, and then serve.

Desserts

Grandma's Apple "Cake" ❖ Old-Fashioned Pound Cake ❖
Apple Bundt Cake ❖ *Schlag* (Fresh Whipped Cream) ❖ Chocolate
Streusel Bundt Cake ❖ Grandma's Cheesecake ❖ Apricot and
Chocolate Tart ❖ *Variation:* Chocolate-Dipped Apricot-Filled Cookies ❖
Harvest "Cake" ❖ Italian Plum Tart ❖ Hazelnut Torte ❖ Delicious Chocolate
Confection with Chocolate Cream ❖ Prunes in White Wine ❖ *Marillenknadel*
(Apricot Dumplings) ❖ Crepes with Cream Cheese Filling and Apricot
Sauce ❖ Chocolate-Chip Matzo Brittle ❖ Butter Horns ❖ Vanilla
Horns ❖ Cinnamon Twists ❖ Fresh Strawberry Sauce

Grandma's Apple "Cake"

MAKES 1 12 BY 7½-INCH PIE

FOR THE SUGAR CRUST
¾ pound (3 sticks) cold unsalted
    margarine
⅔ cup sugar
2 extra-large eggs
1 teaspoon pure vanilla extract
4 cups all-purpose flour

FOR THE FILLING
¾ cup sugar
9 tablespoons apricot preserves
¾ teaspoon ground cinnamon
1½ tablespoons all-purpose
    flour
3 tablespoons cornstarch
3 tablespoons water
12 cups peeled medium-thick
    (½ inch wide) McIntosh
    apple slices (about 12 large
    apples)

Egg wash of 1 extra-large egg,
    beaten lightly
Sugar, for sprinkling on the crust

Here is the "cake" that Oma baked in the morning on Fridays and hid in her bedroom (from mischievous little hands) until she served it at dinner that night. We called it cake and still do despite the fact that it is made with a sugar crust dough and is rightfully a two-crust apple pie. How it came to be called cake, I don't know. I have loved it from the first taste I ever had as a little girl, and I still do.

But there is more significance to this cake than even that. When I opened my bakery, My Most Favorite Dessert Company, in Great Neck, Long Island, in the early 1980s, I started out with products that were mostly American in origin—apple pies, carrot cake, and the like. One day I was thinking of Oma, and her unforgettable apple cake came to mind. From that, I began to ponder my country of birth, Austria, then the years I had spent in Italy as a very young child. That trip back in time was a wonderful awakening for me: I was going back into my past to acknowledge something specifically from my past. Oma and her apple cake had been the inspiration.

I made Oma's cake at my bakery and could not believe how customers reacted to it the first time I offered it for sale: "Oh, my mother made a cake like that," or, "My grandmother's cake!" Some customers even had similar stories of its being hidden by their grandmothers or mothers, just as Oma had stashed it away in her bedroom, safe from Ruth and me. Everyone, it seemed, could relate to it. Fond memories, personal recollections, the baking of generations were wrapped up in this panful of apples in sweet dough. And so it remains.

This recipe appears in my first book, *My Most Favorite Dessert Company Cookbook.* I'm including it here because . . . how could I not?

◈

Make the dough: In the bowl of a standing electric mixer fitted with the paddle attachment, cream the margarine with the sugar on medium speed until fluffy.

In a small bowl, beat the eggs together with the vanilla. With the mixer running, add the egg mixture to the margarine mixture and beat until incorporated.

Reduce the mixer speed to low and add the flour, 1 cup at a time, beating until a ball of dough forms around the paddle.

With your hands gather the dough into a ball. Divide the ball in half, shape each half into a disk, and wrap in plastic wrap. Chill for 2 to 3 hours. (Or make the dough the day before and chill it overnight.)

Preheat the oven to 350 degrees F. Line a large baking sheet with parchment paper and set aside. Remove the disks of dough from the refrigerator and let them stand at room temperature to soften slightly before rolling.

On a lightly floured surface, roll one of the disks of dough into a ¼-inch-thick 14 × 9 inches rectangle. Gently roll the dough over the rolling pin and center it over a 12 × 7½-inch rectangular baking pan. Press the dough over the bottom and up the sides. Trim the overhang so that it covers the rim of the pan. Chill the pie shell while you make the filling.

Make the apple filling mixture: In a large bowl, stir together the sugar, apricot preserves, cinnamon, and flour until well combined.

Put the cornstarch in a small bowl, add the water, and stir until combined and there are no lumps. Stir the cornstarch mixture into the apricot mixture. Add the apple slices, and with your hands, toss until the apples are well coated.

Place the apple filling in the prepared pan, mounding it in the center. (The filling will stand very high in the pan.)

With a pastry brush, brush the edge of the dough all the way around with the egg wash.

Reflour the work surface lightly and roll out the remaining pieces of dough into a ¼-inch-thick 14 × 9-inch rectangle. Roll the dough over the rolling pin and center it over the filling. With your fingers, press the edge of the top crust into the edge of the bottom crust, sealing it at the corners, then all the way around. Trim the edge of the top dough even with the edge of the pan. With the tines of a fork, lightly press the edge of the crust all the way around to seal. Prick the top crust all over with the tines of the fork to make steam vents.

Brush the top crust and the edge with egg wash, then sprinkle generously with sugar.

Place the pan on the lined baking sheet and bake for 1 hour and 5 to 10 minutes until the top crust is a lovely golden brown. Transfer the cake to a wire rack and let it cool completely. You can also serve it warm. Store leftovers, covered with plastic wrap, in the refrigerator for up to 3 days.

OLD-FASHIONED POUND CAKE

MAKES 1 10-INCH CAKE

If my grandmother's signature dish was her apple "cake," my mother's claim to fame in the dessert department was this pound cake, which she made for special occasions. It is not a classic recipe for pound cake, but it is luscious and rich, thanks to equal amounts of cream cheese and butter. If it should last long enough to become slightly stale, don't toss it; toast it. It is exquisite in summer with berries and *Schlag* (Fresh Whipped Cream, page 184).

2¾ cups all-purpose flour

1¼ teaspoons baking powder

6 extra-large eggs

1½ teaspoons fresh lemon juice

1½ teaspoons pure vanilla extract

½ pound (2 sticks) unsalted butter, softened

½ pound cream cheese, at room temperature

2 cups sugar

Preheat the oven to 350 degrees F. Grease and flour a 10-inch fluted tube pan and set aside.

In a medium bowl, whisk together the flour and baking powder. Into another bowl, break the eggs, then add the lemon juice and vanilla, without stirring.

In the bowl of a standing electric mixer fitted with the paddle attachment, cream the butter with the cream cheese and sugar on medium-low speed until light and fluffy. Slowly add the egg mixture, beating until well blended. Scrape down the sides of the bowl with a rubber spatula, then add the flour mixture and beat on low speed until all the flour is incorporated and the batter is smooth.

Scrape the batter into the prepared pan and smooth the top. Bake for about 1 hour, or until a cake tester inserted in the center comes out clean. Transfer the pan to a wire rack and let the cake cool for 10 minutes. Unmold the cake onto the rack and let cool completely before cutting into slices.

Store the pound cake, wrapped tightly in plastic wrap, at room temperature.

APPLE BUNDT CAKE

MAKES 1 10-INCH CAKE

O ma liked baking with apples. Here is another apple cake of hers. It is good with a cup of tea or coffee in the afternoon, but I like it best for dessert.

Preheat the oven to 350 degrees F. Grease and flour a 10-inch Kugelhopf pan and set aside.

In a bowl, whisk together the flour and baking powder. In a cup, stir together the orange juice and vanilla.

In the bowl of an electric mixer fitted with the paddle attachment, cream the margarine and 1½ cups sugar until light and fluffy. Beat in the eggs, one at a time, beating well after each addition. Add the flour mixture to the beaten egg mixture in thirds, alternating with the orange juice mixture, and combine the batter well.

In another bowl, toss the chopped apples with the ⅔ cup sugar, cinnamon, and orange zest.

Pour half of the batter into the prepared pan and top it with half of the apple mixture. Cover the apples with the remaining batter and top with the remaining apple mixture.

Bake the cake for 1 hour, or until a cake tester inserted in the center comes out clean. Transfer the cake to a wire rack to cool completely.

To serve, invert the cake onto a platter.

2¼ cups all-purpose flour

2¼ teaspoons baking powder

¼ cup orange juice

2½ teaspoons pure vanilla extract

½ pound (2 sticks) unsalted margarine

1½ cups plus ⅔ cup sugar

3 extra-large eggs

4 medium McIntosh apples, peeled, cored, and roughly chopped

1 teaspoon ground cinnamon

1 teaspoon grated orange zest

SCHLAG

(Fresh Whipped Cream)

MAKES ABOUT 2 CUPS

1 cup well-chilled heavy cream
½ teaspoon pure vanilla extract
2 tablespoons sugar

My mother used to love to go to Rumpelmayer's on Central Park South for hot coffee with a scoop of ice cream floated on the top. That elegant restaurant, with its European-style desserts, coffees, chocolates, and sparkling chandeliers, reminded Berta of Vienna and the stylish *konditorei* there. Our visits to Rumpelmayer's made her truly happy.

Fresh whipped cream, *schlag*, makes me content in the same way Berta's special cup of coffee did her. It is something I love. What could be better than a spoonful or two of this in coffee, or as an accompaniment to pastry, any pastry?

In a large bowl, combine the cream and vanilla. With an electric mixer on medium speed, beat until the cream is foamy. Beating, add the sugar in a slow, steady stream and beat until the cream just holds soft, billowy peaks. Take care not to overbeat. The cream should stand in soft mounds. Spoon into a serving bowl and serve.

CHOCOLATE STREUSEL BUNDT CAKE

MAKES 1 10-INCH CAKE

This coffee cake is moist and studded with layers of chocolate-nut streusel, with more streusel on top. It is delicious for dessert, with fresh fruit. Slice it gently; too much pressure on the knife will cause the streusel layers to separate from the crumb.

❖

Preheat the oven to 350 degrees F. Generously grease a 9-inch Bundt pan and set aside.

Prepare the streusel: In a bowl, stir together the brown sugar, flour, cocoa powder, and ground spices. Add the butter and work it with your fingertips or two knives until it resembles pea-sized pieces. Add the chocolate and pecans.

Make the cake: In a large bowl, stir together the flour, cocoa powder, baking powder, baking soda, salt, and cinnamon.

In a bowl with an electric mixer, cream the butter and brown sugar on medium speed until light and fluffy. Beat in the eggs, one at a time, beating well after each addition. Scrape down the sides of the bowl with a spatula, and stir in the sour cream and vanilla until incorporated.

Add the egg mixture to the dry ingredients, stirring to combine. Do not overmix.

Scatter 1 cup of the streusel mixture over the bottom of

FOR THE STREUSEL
¾ cup packed light brown sugar
¼ cup all-purpose flour
1½ tablespoons unsweetened cocoa powder
¼ teaspoon ground cinnamon
¼ teaspoon ground nutmeg
4 tablespoons (½ stick) chilled unsalted butter, cut into pieces
1 cup chopped semisweet chocolate
1 cup finely chopped pecans

FOR THE CAKE
1¾ cups all-purpose flour
¼ cup unsweetened cocoa powder
2 teaspoons baking powder
½ teaspoon baking soda
½ teaspoon salt
¼ teaspoon ground cinnamon
8 tablespoons (1 stick) unsalted butter, softened
¾ cup packed light brown sugar
3 extra-large eggs
1 cup sour cream
2 teaspoons pure vanilla extract

the prepared pan. Top with one third of the batter, and level the top, taking care not to disturb the layer of streusel beneath. Scatter half of the remaining streusel over the batter, and top with half of the remaining batter. Level this layer of batter carefully. Make one more layer of streusel and batter and level the top. (There should be no streusel left.)

Bake the cake 45 to 50 minutes, or until a cake tester inserted in the center comes out clean. Transfer the cake to a wire rack, let stand for 5 minutes, and invert onto the rack to cool.

To store, wrap the cake in plastic wrap and store it in the refrigerator for up to 5 days. For the best flavor, return the cake to room temperature before serving.

Grandma's Cheesecake

MAKES 1 12 BY 7½-INCH CAKE

This is cheesecake in the Austrian style, with a crust on both the bottom and the top. It is not overly sweet, as American cheesecake sometimes is.

"This is the cheesecake I dream about!" exclaimed my friend Rita at the first bite. Rita had been born in Vienna and was living there when her family fled to Cuba before eventually coming to the United States to live. Another Austrian-born friend at the dinner that night took a piece of this cake home. And my cousin Ruth, who remembers living in Vienna before her family also escaped, said: *"This is the cake."*

Make the dough: In the bowl of an electric mixer fitted with the paddle attachment, cream the butter and sugar on medium speed until fluffy. Beat in the egg until incorporated. Reduce the speed to low, and add the flour slowly, beating until a ball of dough forms around the paddle. Remove the dough from the bowl, shape it in a disk, wrap it in plastic wrap, and chill for at least 1 hour.

Make the filling: In the mixer, combine the eggs and sugar until well blended. Add the cottage cheese and blend until just incorporated. Add the farina and lemon zest. Stir in the raisins until evenly distributed.

Preheat the oven to 350 degrees F.

FOR THE CRUST

12 tablespoons (1½ sticks)
    unsalted butter, softened
⅓ cup sugar
1 extra-large egg
2 cups all-purpose flour, plus
    additional, for rolling

FOR THE FILLING

5 extra-large eggs, beaten lightly
1 cup sugar
1½ pounds large-curd creamed
    cottage cheese, or ricotta
    cheese
Grated zest of 1 lemon
¼ cup regular farina
½ cup golden raisins
1 egg white, beaten lightly,
    for egg wash
Sugar, for sprinkling on the crust

Divide the dough in half. On a lightly floured surface, roll one piece of the dough into a rectangle to fit a 12 × 7½-inch baking pan, with a slight overhang. Roll the dough over the rolling pin, center it over the pan, unroll, and line the bottom and sides, pressing the dough gently into the corners. Spoon the cheese filling into the pan and level the surface. Lightly reflour the surface and roll the remaining piece of dough into a rectangle to cover the pan and center it over the filling. Press the bottom overhang up and over the edge of the top crust. Crimp to seal the edges together. Brush the top crust and edges of the dough with the beaten egg white and sprinkle the top of the crust with sugar. Prick the top crust all over with the tines of a fork.

Bake the cheesecake until the crust is a lovely golden brown, about 40 minutes. Transfer the cake to a wire rack to cool.

To serve, cut the cake into squares. Store the cake, covered with plastic wrap, in the refrigerator for 3 to 5 days. If chilled, warm the cake in a preheated 200-degree oven for 3 to 6 minutes, just to take the chill off.

APRICOT AND CHOCOLATE TART

MAKES 1 8-INCH TART

The combination of apricots and chocolate, both of which I love, struck a Viennese chord in me, and so I decided to pair them as the filling in this lattice-topped tart.

You will have a bit of dough left over after you line the pan. Save it to make the most delicious sandwich cookies you can imagine. They're also filled with apricot preserves, but then you coat them entirely in melted chocolate. They are the kind of European-style cookie Oma loved.

Make the dough: In the bowl of an electric mixer fitted with the paddle attachment, cream the butter and the sugar on medium speed until fluffy and lemon colored. Add the egg and beat until incorporated. Reduce the speed to low, add the flour, and beat until a ball of dough forms around the paddle. Remove the dough from the bowl, shape it into a disk, wrap it in plastic wrap, and chill for 2 to 3 hours, until firm.

Preheat the oven to 350 degrees F. Remove the dough from the refrigerator to soften slightly.

Divide the dough in half. On a lightly floured surface, roll one piece of the dough into a 9-inch round, about ⅛ inch thick. Roll the dough over the rolling pin, center it over an 8-inch tart pan with a removable bottom, and

FOR THE DOUGH
12 tablespoons (1½ sticks) unsalted butter, softened

⅓ cup sugar

1 extra-large egg

2 cups all-purpose flour, plus additional, for rolling

FOR THE FILLING
1½ cups apricot preserves

¼ cup chopped semisweet chocolate

1 tablespoon grated orange zest

1 extra-large egg, beaten lightly, for egg wash

gently press the dough into the pan and up the sides (there will be an overhang). Roll the pin over the top edge of the pan to trim the dough. Press the scraps into a disk and reserve.

Make the filling: In a bowl, stir together all of the filling ingredients.

Spread the filling over the dough in the pan (the filling should come almost to the top of the pan).

Lightly reflour the surface, and roll out the remaining piece of dough into a 9-inch round, about ¼ inch thick. With a sharp knife (or a pizza cutter) and a ruler, cut 8 strips, each about ¾ inch wide. Lay 4 of the strips across the top of the tart, spacing them evenly, and press the edges of the strips firmly into the side of the dough. Place the 4 remaining strips at right angles on top of the first strips to create a latticework pattern, pressing them firmly onto the sides. Combine the scraps with those left over from the bottom crust, press them into a ball, wrap in plastic wrap, and chill.

With a pastry brush, brush the strips and the top edge of the tart with the egg wash.

Bake the tart for about 40 minutes, until the pastry is golden and the sides of the tart have pulled slightly away from the edge of the pan. Transfer the tart to a wire rack and let cool completely.

Remove the sides of the pan before placing the tart on a plate to serve.

CHOCOLATE-DIPPED APRICOT-FILLED COOKIES

MAKES ABOUT 8 SANDWICH COOKIES

Preheat the oven to 350 degrees F.

On a lightly floured surface, roll the dough out ⅛ inch thick. With a 2¼-inch round cookie cutter, cut out 16 rounds. Transfer the rounds to a baking sheet and bake for 10 to 12 minutes, until just golden. Remove to a wire rack to cool. (You may have an extra round. Bake it and enjoy eating it!)

When cool, brush 8 of the rounds with a dab or two of apricot preserves. Cover each with one of the plain cookies.

Melt the chocolate in a small saucepan over low heat, stirring until smooth and glossy. Dip the cookies, one at a time, into the melted chocolate, coating half of it well, and letting the excess drip back into the pan. Stand the cookies, uncoated side down, in a container, put the container in the freezer, and let the chocolate harden. Dip the other half of each cookie in the melted chocolate and dry in the same manner.

Reserved dough from making Apricot and Chocolate Tart (page 189)

Apricot preserves

6 ounces chopped semisweet chocolate, melted

HARVEST "CAKE"

MAKES 1 12 BY 7½-INCH CAKE

FOR THE DOUGH

10 tablespoons (1¼ sticks)
   unsalted butter, softened

1 cup sugar

1 extra-large egg

3 extra-large egg yolks

½ cup orange juice

Grated zest of 1 lemon

3¼ cups all-purpose flour, plus
   additional, for rolling

2½ teaspoons baking powder

Apricot preserves, for brushing
   the dough

FOR THE FILLING

3 cups peeled, cored, and
   chopped McIntosh apples
   (4 medium)

1 cup chopped blanched
   lmonds, or other nut of
   choice

½ cup chopped dried dates

½ cup chopped dried figs

¼ cup sugar

Grated zest of 2 lemons
   (2 tablespoons)

1 tablespoon fresh lemon juice

1 teaspoon ground cinnamon

1 extra-large egg white, beaten
   lightly, for egg wash

2 tablespoons sugar, for
   sprinkling on the crust

I am always looking for new desserts for My Most Favorite Dessert Company, and this is a variation on the theme of my most favorite dessert of all: Grandma's Apple "Cake" (page 178). I used a different dough, and added figs, dates, and nuts to Oma's basic apple filling. The result is somewhat exotic and different thanks to the dried fruits.

Serve this on Succoth or on Thanksgiving (for a festive menu, see page 242). If you observe the dietary laws, simply substitute the same amount of unsalted margarine for the butter when making the crust.

Make the dough: In the bowl of an electric mixer fitted with the paddle attachment, cream the butter and sugar on medium speed until fluffy. Beat in the egg, egg yolks, orange juice, and lemon zest until incorporated.

In a bowl, whisk together the flour and baking powder.

Reduce the speed to low and add the flour mixture, one cup at a time, beating until a ball of dough forms around the paddle. Gather the dough into a ball, divide it into 2 equal pieces, and pat each into a flat disk. Wrap each piece in plastic wrap and chill in the refrigerator for up to 4 hours (but at least 2 hours), or until firm.

Preheat the oven to 350 degrees F.

On a lightly floured surface, roll one piece of the

dough into a rectangle to fit a 12 × 7½-inch baking pan, with a slight overhang. Roll the dough over the rolling pin, center it over the pan, and line the bottom and sides, pressing the dough gently into the corners. Brush the bottom and sides of the dough with a layer of apricot preserves.

Make the filling: In a large bowl, combine all the filling ingredients, stirring well. Spread the filling in an even layer over the dough in the pan.

Lightly reflour the work surface and roll the remaining piece of dough into a rectangle to cover the pan. Center the dough over the filling. Trim the overhanging dough with the edge of the pan, then crimp the sides decoratively all the way around to seal. Brush the top of the dough with the beaten egg white and sprinkle with sugar. Prick the top crust all over with the tines of a fork.

Place the pan on a baking sheet and bake for 50 minutes to 1 hour, or until the pastry is golden in color. Transfer the pan to a wire rack and let cool completely before serving.

THE FAMILY WORK ETHIC

If you consider the "job" Oma took on after coming to the United States, heading up our household, which, in turn, enabled her daughters and son-in-law to go to work every day, Oma herself worked from her twenties (in Vienna) into her late sixties (here). My mother and her sister, Ciel, worked for decades, too. My mother worked into her eighties and she took the subway to work every day.

As for myself, I go to My Most Favorite Dessert Company every day and have done so for years. I don't see changing that anytime soon. Why? It is an inherited trait Oma instilled in us right from the start: After family, there was nothing more important than to participate in the world.

Italian Plum Tart

MAKES 1 10-INCH TART

There are two important things to remember about this recipe: Italian plums, with their unique purply-blue color and sugary flavor, are available only in the fall. Secondly, the crust I have called for below makes more than you need. In fact, you will have enough crust for two 10-inch tarts. You have several options: (1) Make two tarts, which will require doubling the filling ingredients; (2) Freeze the remaining dough to use at another time; (3) Or my favorite, invite your grandchildren over to bake cookies, then have a little party with them.

Flour, for rolling Harvest "Cake" dough (page 192), made up to the point of chilling
Flour, for rolling
12 Italian plums
½ cup sugar
½ teaspoon ground cinnamon
4 tablespoons (½ stick) unsalted butter or unsalted margarine, melted and cooled

Divide the dough into 2 pieces and wrap as directed. Chill one of the pieces until firm, a minimum of 2 hours. Freeze the remaining piece, or use as suggested above.

Preheat the oven to 350 degrees F.

On a lightly floured surface, roll the dough into an 11-inch round. Center it over the middle of a 10-inch pan with a removable bottom, and press it over the bottom and up the sides. Roll the pin over the rim of the pan to trim the edge.

Cut each of the plums in half and remove the pit. Cut each half into ¼-inch slices *without* cutting all the way through the skin. (The halves when cut should "fan." You do not want separate plum slices.)

Arrange the plum halves, cut side up, in the lined tart

shell, starting at the outside edge and proceeding clockwise, until the entire shell is filled. It is very important to place the halves as close together as possible. When you get to the center of the tart, the halves will begin to overlap and that is fine. Do not trim them to fit. The closer the plum halves are, the better, as they will shrink during baking.

Combine the sugar with the cinnamon and sprinkle over the plums. Drizzle the melted butter over the sugared plums.

Place the tart on a baking sheet and bake for 50 to 60 minutes, or until the plums are softened and the pastry is deep golden. Remove to a wire rack to cool.

Before serving, remove the sides of the pan. The tart can be covered in plastic wrap and stored in the refrigerator for 3 days.

Hazelnut Torte

MAKES 1 8-INCH CAKE

This cake is superb served with a fresh fruit sauce or puree on Passover. (My preference, is strawberry.) For a complete Passover menu, see page 236.

Note below that the hazelnuts are not skinned (such a chore!), but they are toasted. To toast them, spread the nuts in a single layer on a small baking sheet and bake them at 350 degrees F. for 15 to 20 minutes, stirring them halfway through the baking time. Let cool, then grind in a food processor.

❖

1 cup hazelnuts, toasted, *not* skinned, and finely ground
⅓ cup matzo cake meal, plus extra, for dusting the pan
1 teaspoon potato starch
1 extra-large whole egg
6 extra-large eggs, separated
¾ cup granulated sugar
Confectioner's sugar, for dusting
Fresh Strawberry Sauce (page 215)

Preheat the oven to 350 degrees F. Grease an 8-inch round cake pan, dust it with matzo cake meal, shaking out the excess and set aside.

In a bowl, whisk together the ground hazelnuts, cake meal, and potato starch until combined.

In a large bowl with an electric mixer, beat the whole egg and the 6 egg yolks on medium speed until thick and light yellow in color. Add ½ cup of the granulated sugar and beat until combined and light lemon in color. Add the hazelnut mixture, and mix on low speed until combined.

In the bowl of an electric mixer fitted with the whisk attachment, beat the 6 egg whites on medium speed until foamy. Gradually add the remaining ¼ cup granulated sugar, increase the speed to medium-high, and beat until the whites hold stiff peaks. Stir one-quarter of the beaten whites into the nut batter to lighten it, then with a large rubber spatula fold the remaining whites gently in until no streaks of white remain.

Scrape the batter into the prepared cake pan, level the top, and bake for 40 to 45 minutes, or until a cake tester inserted in the center comes out with no crumbs attached. Transfer the cake to a wire rack and let it cool in the pan before inverting it onto a serving plate.

Just before serving, dust the top with confectioner's sugar. Pass the Strawberry Sauce at the table.

Delicious Chocolate Confection with Chocolate Cream

MAKES 1 10-INCH CAKE

Many of the recipes in this book were inspired by Oma, others by my mother, some are my own, and then there is this one, which was given to me by a very kind stranger. One summer, years ago, we were at the Tanglewood Music Festival, where I met a lovely woman from . . . Vienna. Somehow we got on the subject of food and baking, in particular, perhaps in response to my having mentioned my bakery and restaurant. She said that she had a recipe for flourless chocolate cake and added that I could call her for it the next day, but with the proviso not to disturb her until after ten in the morning. This is that cake, and it was well worth waiting for.

If you observe the dietary laws, the cake is appropriate for serving on Passover, but with a menu that includes meat, will need to be accompanied by Fresh Strawberry Sauce (page 215) or a puree of raspberries. At other times, garnish it as my Viennese acquaintance gave it to me below, with its rich chocolate whipped cream. Note that the cream is made with uncooked egg yolks.

❖

Preheat the oven to 350 degrees F. Grease a 10-inch round cake pan and set aside.

FOR THE CONFECTION BATTER

6 ounces semisweet chocolate bits

¾ cup plus 2 tablespoons sugar

½ cup water

1⅓ cups finely ground walnuts

7 extra-large eggs, separated

FOR THE CHOCOLATE CREAM

4 ounces semisweet chocolate bits

¼ cup black coffee

1 cup chilled heavy cream

4 extra-large egg yolks

Make the confection batter: In a medium saucepan, melt the chocolate bits with the sugar and the water over very low heat, stirring. Add the nuts, stirring to combine well, and remove the pan from the heat. Transfer the chocolate mixture to a large bowl to cool. When cool, whisk in the egg yolks, one at a time, whisking well after each addition.

In a large bowl, beat the egg whites with an electric mixer on high speed until they hold stiff peaks. Fold the beaten whites gently but thoroughly into the chocolate mixture until no traces of white remain.

Pour the batter into the prepared pan and level the top. Bake for 40 to 50 minutes, until the cake is crusty on top and light brown in color. Turn off the oven, but leave the cake in the turned-off oven with the door open for 30 minutes. Transfer the pan to a wire rack and allow to cool completely.

Make the chocolate cream: In a small saucepan, melt the chocolate bits with the coffee over very low heat, stirring. Remove the pan from the heat and let cool.

In a medium bowl with the electric mixer, beat the heavy cream on medium-high speed to soft peaks.

Stir the egg yolks, one at a time, into the cooled chocolate mixture, whisking well after each addition. Fold in the whipped cream gently but thoroughly. Spoon the cream into a serving bowl.

To serve, invert the confection onto a serving plate. Cut it into slices and garnish each serving with a spoonful or two of the chocolate cream. Pass the remaining chocolate cream separately.

PRUNES IN WHITE WINE

MAKES 6 TO 8 SMALL SERVINGS

I use sweet white kosher wine for poaching these prunes, which results in an out-of-this-world syrup. A delicate cookie, Vanilla Horns (page 211), for example, makes the perfect accompaniment. If you refer to the menus that begin on page 227, you will see that I have suggested this dessert for several different venues. Why? It is easy to prepare, refreshing, and must be made in advance.

1 pound (16 ounces) pitted whole prunes
1 bottle sweet kosher white wine, as in Joyvin White
1 cinnamon stick, 3 to 4 inches long
¼ cup sugar

In a medium-large saucepan, combine all the ingredients. Cover and cook over medium heat for 10 minutes. Remove the cover and simmer slowly 30 to 35 minutes longer, until the wine is reduced by about three-quarters and the prunes still hold their shape but are very soft. Transfer the fruit and cooking syrup to a serving bowl, remove the cinnamon stick, if desired, and let cool. Cover with plastic wrap and chill until serving time.

MARILLENKNADEL

(Apricot Dumplings)

MAKES 16 DUMPLINGS

FOR THE DOUGH

2 pounds baking (Idaho)
    potatoes, peeled

4 tablespoons (½ stick)
    unsalted butter

1 whole extra-large egg

1 extra-large egg yolk

About 2½ cups all-purpose
    flour, plus additional as
    needed and for rolling

16 ready-to-eat, really ripe
    apricots

16 sugar cubes

FOR THE CRUMBS

8 tablespoons (1 stick) unsalted
    butter

2½ cups Homemade Bread
    Crumbs (page 62)

¼ cup sugar

You wouldn't have believed the response these dumplings evoked when I made them one day for family and friends who have connections to Austria and Hungary. Everyone there had a fond memory or a story about *Marillenknadel*, myself included. My sister and I had taken our mother to Vienna in the late 1990s. A short river trip, by boat, took us to a small town called Melk. In a restaurant there we had these dumplings. I will never forget how good they were—or how my sister told me at the time not to eat too many of them! That reminded me of an anecdote my Viennese friend Elisabeth related: Apparently children in Austria compete to see how many of these they can eat. I would have loved a contest like that as a child . . . and as a grown-up, too.

There are a number of ways to serve these: For a wonderful summer meal, with soup and deviled eggs beforehand; as a meal in themselves; or, as we did in Melk, with just a bowl of soup beforehand.

You can also make these dumplings with plums or with sweetened strawberries.

◆

For the dough: Place the potatoes in a large pot and cover them with cold water. Bring the water to a boil over medium-high heat and boil the potatoes for 15 to 20 minutes, or until fork-tender. Drain and transfer them to a potato ricer, and rice them into a large bowl. Stir the butter into the potatoes until melted and fully incorporated. Stir in the whole egg and egg yolk until blended. Slowly add 2 cups of the flour, stirring until a dough forms. If the dough is sticky, add additional flour, a little at a time, up to ½ cup total, until the dough feels elastic and smooth, and no longer tacky to the touch. Cover the bowl with plastic wrap and let it stand at room temperature while you prepare the apricots.

Pit the apricots, then fill each of the cavities with a sugar cube.

Meanwhile, bring an 8-quart pot of water to a boil.

Lightly dust a countertop or large flat surface with flour. Form the dough into a disk, flatten it with your hands, and roll it into a square ¼ to ⅛ inch thick. With a ruler and a sharp knife, cut 16 equally sized squares in the dough. Center an apricot in the middle of each dough square, then mold the dough up and over the fruit, sealing it completely. If the dough becomes sticky, roll the dumpling lightly in flour and set aside while you make the remaining dumplings.

Make the crumbs: Melt the butter in a large skillet over low heat. Add 1 cup of the bread crumbs and toast them, stirring frequently, until they begin to separate and deepen in color. Add another cup of crumbs and toast them, stirring in the same way. Add the remaining ½ cup crumbs and cook, stirring, until the crumbs are golden brown in color, with no clumps, about 10 minutes. (The stirring is very important because it keeps the crumbs from clumping and burning.) Remove the pan from the heat. Sprinkle the sugar over the crumbs and stir until incorporated.

When the water is at a gentle boil, drop 8 dumplings into the pot. They will immediately sink to the bottom. Boil the dumplings until they pop to the surface, 8 to 10 minutes. With a slotted spoon, transfer the cooked dumplings to the toasted crumbs, and roll them in the crumbs to cover them completely. Serve this first batch of dumplings immediately.

While your guests eat, cook and crumb the remaining dumplings.

Crepes with Cream Cheese Filling and Apricot Sauce

MAKES 16 TO 18 CREPES

These are delicious served either for dessert or for brunch. My husband likes them hot, in which case you simply melt butter or margarine in a skillet, add the crepes (already filled), and sauté them, turning, for several minutes.

If you are a veteran crepe maker, you know that the first few are not always perfect when they come out of the pan. Take a lesson from Oma: Keep at it—the ones following will be fine.

❖

Make the crepe batter: In a blender, combine all the batter ingredients until combined. Put the container in the refrigerator and let the batter chill for at least 30 minutes. Stir before using.

Heat an 8-inch crepe or omelet pan over medium heat with enough butter to just coat the pan when melted. When the pan is hot and the butter has stopped foaming, pour in a ladleful (3 to 4 tablespoons), tilting the pan to cover the bottom. Cook until set on the bottom, I minute. Turn with a spatula or your fingertips and cook until set on the second side. Let cool in a single layer on a sheet of

FOR THE CREPE BATTER
1 cup all-purpose flour

2 tablespoons sugar

Pinch coarse kosher salt

3 extra-large eggs

1 cup milk

1 cup water

2 tablespoons unsalted butter, melted and cooled

FOR THE FILLING
1 cup large-curd creamed cottage cheese

½ cup sour cream

2 tablespoons sugar

1 teaspoon pure vanilla extract

¼ teaspoon grated orange zest

¼ teaspoon grated lemon zest

Unsalted butter or unsalted margarine, for cooking

Apricot Sauce (page 207)

parchment paper. Continue to make crepes with the batter and butter in the same manner.

Make the filling: In a bowl, stir together all the ingredients until well combined.

Fill and wrap the crepes: Spoon the cheese filling in the center of each crepe, then fold the bottom of the crepe up and over to cover the filling. Fold in each of the sides and roll up the crepe. Transfer the crepe, seam side down, to a plate. Fill and wrap the remaining crepes in the same manner, arranging them in a single layer on the plate.

Serve, drizzled with Apricot Sauce.

Apricot Sauce

MAKES 1 CUP

This is the sauce I serve with Crepes with Cream Cheese Filling, although Fresh Strawberry Sauce (page 215) is another good option. I also like the combination of this sauce with Hazelnut Torte (page 197).

⅔ cup apricot preserves

⅓ cup orange juice

2 tablespoons unsalted butter

1½ teaspoons grated lemon zest

1 tablespoon fresh lemon juice

In a small saucepan, combine all the ingredients over low heat, stirring until the butter and jam are melted and the sauce is well combined.

Pour the sauce into a serving bowl, let cool, then chill until ready to serve.

Chocolate-Chip Matzo Brittle

5 sheets of matzo

½ pound (2 sticks) unsalted margarine

1 cup packed brown sugar

1 bag (12 ounces) semisweet chocolate bits, regular size or miniature

My friend Susan has always had a supply of fun recipes. Some people have called them fun *and* addictive. I now know what they mean by addictive. Once you try this brittle, you will not be able to stop noshing on it. For that reason I have not included a yield. You will need 5 matzos (at least). How long your brittle lasts is anyone's guess!

Preheat the oven to 350 degrees F. Line a baking sheet with parchment paper or aluminum foil.

Cover the prepared baking sheet with the matzos. They will overlap and that is fine.

In a medium saucepan, melt the margarine with the sugar until the mixture comes to a boil. (Be careful because the mixture will be very hot.) Pour the sugar mixture evenly over the matzos on the baking sheet. Do this as evenly as you can. Bake for 7 minutes.

Remove the baking sheet from the oven and sprinkle the chocolate bits evenly over the matzos. Return the sheet to the oven for about 2 minutes, until the chips are softened and starting to melt, but not completely melted. Immediately put the baking sheet in the refrigerator to chill.

When the brittle is cool, break it into uneven pieces. Serve in a wide bowl or on a serving plate.

BUTTER HORNS

MAKES 34 COOKIES

This is the type of cookie Oma loved—Old World and refined. Even making these is something of a step back in time, involving in a wonderful kind of way. First you prepare dough. Then you spread it with apricot preserves and a dusting of walnuts, roll it up, cut it into bite-size pieces, glaze them, and bake them. The result of your effort is a European-style cookie—pretty and pleasing—one on display in a pastry shop on a *strasse* in Vienna.

If you observe the dietary laws, use margarine for the butter and soy milk for the cream in the dough.

❖

Make the dough: In a food processor fitted with the metal blade, or by hand, in a large bowl, combine all the ingredients, processing or creaming until a dough forms. Shape the dough into a disk, wrap it in plastic wrap, and refrigerate overnight. The following day, remove the dough from the refrigerator to soften at room temperature.

Preheat the oven to 350 degrees F. Line 2 baking sheets with parchment paper and set aside.

Make the filling: In a small bowl, stir together the sugar, walnuts, and cinnamon.

On a floured surface, roll the dough into a rectangle 27 inches long × 13 inches wide. Spread the apricot jam over the dough, then sprinkle it with the walnut mixture.

FOR THE DOUGH

Scant 2½ cups all-purpose flour, plus additional, for rolling

16 tablespoons (2 sticks) unsalted butter, softened

4 extra-large egg yolks

Pinch salt

3 tablespoons heavy cream

FOR THE FILLING

⅓ cup sugar

Scant ¾ cup finely chopped walnuts

½ teaspoon ground cinnamon

6 tablespoons apricot preserves

1 extra-large egg white, beaten lightly, for egg wash

½ teaspoon ground cinnamon combined with ¼ cup sugar

With a pizza cutter or sharp knife and a ruler, cut the dough lengthwise into 2 equal pieces. Starting with a long side, roll up each piece of dough jelly-roll fashion, pressing the seam on each roll gently to seal. With a pastry brush, brush each log with some of the beaten egg white, then sprinkle each with cinnamon sugar. With a sharp knife, cut each log into pieces 1½ inches long. (You should have 17 pieces per log.) Divide the pieces between the prepared baking sheets, leaving 1 inch or so in between.

Bake for 20 to 30 minutes, until the cookies are golden brown. Transfer the cookies to wire racks to cool. Store in layers separated by wax paper in an airtight container for 1 week.

Vanilla Horns

MAKES 60 TO 75 COOKIES, DEPENDING ON SIZE

My aunt Ciel, my mother's younger sister, was beautiful, accomplished as a businesswoman, and sophisticated. Later in life, Ciel developed an interest in baking and one day mentioned to Oma that she was going to bake peanut butter cookies. The look of horror that crossed Oma's face was unforgettable. *Peanut butter?* For Oma, the very notion was unthinkable. The only cookies worth baking, from Oma's point of view, were made with butter, finely ground nuts, and powdery sugar—like these.

These cookies are delicate beyond belief. No one I know can stop at one. But then again—and begging to differ with Oma—that can be said of a good peanut butter cookie, too!

16 tablespoons (2 sticks)
    unsalted butter, softened
½ cup granulated sugar
2 teaspoons pure vanilla extract
2¼ cups all-purpose flour
1 cup finely ground almonds,
    with or without the skins
Confectioner's sugar, for dusting

Preheat the oven to 350 degrees F.

In the bowl of an electric mixer fitted with the paddle attachment, cream the butter with the granulated sugar on medium speed until light and fluffy. Beat in the vanilla.

In a bowl, whisk together the flour and almonds.

With the mixer on low speed, add the flour mixture to the butter mixture and blend just until a dough forms around the paddle. Break off generous teaspoonful amounts of the dough, form into a horn or crescent shape, and arrange on a baking sheet, leaving 1 inch in between. Bake for 10 to 15 minutes, until lightly golden. Do not overbake.

With a spatula, remove the cookies to a wire rack to cool completely. Spoon confectioner's sugar into a fine sieve or sifter and lightly dust the cookies with the sugar. Store in layers separated by wax paper in an airtight container for 1 week.

My aunt Ciel in her young and glamorous days.

Cinnamon Twists

MAKES ABOUT 44 COOKIES, EACH 7 INCHES LONG

These unusual cookies are shaped like twisted bread-sticks, and look especially appealing when served in a high-sided glass cylinder—a vase works nicely. Not too sweet, they can be addictive served with a cup of coffee with *Schlag* (page 184).

❖

Preheat the oven to 350 degrees F. Line 2 baking sheets with parchment paper.

In a large bowl, whisk together the flour and baking powder until combined.

In the bowl of an electric mixer fitted with the paddle attachment, cream the butter with I cup of the sugar until light and fluffy. Add the eggs, one at a time, beating well after each addition. Stir in the vanilla. With the mixer on low speed, add the dry ingredients and beat until a dough forms.

Make the cinnamon sugar: In a bowl, stir together the remaining ½ cup sugar and cinnamon, then spread it evenly over a baking sheet or a flat surface.

To shape the twists: Measure the dough into tablespoons. Shape each tablespoon into a compact cylinder, about 2 inches long, then roll it with your hands on a counter top until it measures 12 inches. Fold the roll in half, then twist the

3¾ cups all-purpose flour

2 teaspoons baking powder

8 tablespoons (1 stick) unsalted butter, softened

1½ cups sugar

3 extra-large eggs

2 teaspoons pure vanilla extract

1½ teaspoons ground cinnamon

roll about 3 times to form a spiral. Roll the spiral gently in the cinnamon sugar, coating it completely as you maintain the spiral "rope-y" shape. (When you roll the spiral in the sugar mixture, it will lengthen by about 1 inch.) Transfer each finished twist to the prepared baking sheet, leaving about ½ inch in between. Continue to make twists and sugar them in the same manner.

Bake the twists one sheet at a time for 15 minutes, until lightly golden. Let cool on the baking sheet, then transfer to a wire rack to cool completely. Store the twists in a large container in layers separated by wax paper for 1 week.

FRESH STRAWBERRY SAUCE

MAKES ABOUT 2½ CUPS

There is something very appealing about the texture and taste of this homemade sauce. The berries retain a bit of their shape and the flavor is true and fruity, and not overly sweet.

Serve this with Old-Fashioned Pound Cake (page 181) and *Schlag* (page 184) for a summertime treat, or with Crepes with Cream Cheese Filling (page 205), either in addition to the suggested Apricot Sauce or as a variation.

1 pint ripe strawberries, hulled

1 cup water

¼ cup sugar

❖

In a medium saucepan, combine all the ingredients and bring to a simmer over medium heat. Simmer gently, uncovered, stirring occasionally, for 15 minutes, until the liquid is syrupy and the strawberries have cooked down but still hold some shape. Transfer the sauce to a serving bowl and let cool. Store in an airtight container in the refrigerator for 3 days.

SAUCES, A CHUTNEY, A RUB, AND AN OIL

Apple-Horseradish Sauce ❖ Cucumber-Dill Sauce ❖ Applesauce ❖ Tomato
Sauce ❖ Cranberry-Fig Chutney ❖ Sage and Rosemary Rub ❖ Garlic Oil

APPLE-HORSERADISH SAUCE

MAKES A GENEROUS 2 CUPS

1 jar (6 ounces) Gold's Prepared Horseradish

1 jar (6 ounces) Gold's Prepared Horseradish and Beets

1 cup sugar

2 medium McIntosh apples

This is *the* horseradish sauce I serve with Gefilte Fish (page 23) and Brisket (page 69)—two important dishes in both Oma's household and my own. The grated apple makes it especially delicious.

If two cups is too much for your needs, halve the amounts.

In a medium glass or ceramic bowl, combine the white and red horseradish. Add the sugar and stir to dissolve.

Peel, core, and grate the apples. Add the grated apples to the horseradish mixture and stir until well combined. Cover the bowl with plastic wrap and chill until serving time.

CUCUMBER-DILL SAUCE

MAKES ABOUT 2 CUPS

I cannot remember if Oma served her Fried Flounder (page 123) with a sauce. But I like to, especially if the flounder is hot out of the pan and the sauce is well chilled. The combination of cucumbers, dill, and mayonnaise goes naturally with my Fresh Salmon Cakes (page 122), too.

Don't think of this sauce just with fish, though; it can be used as a salad dressing—on wedges of iceberg lettuce, like the dressing on a steakhouse salad.

2 large seedless cucumbers

½ teaspoon coarse kosher salt

1 cup mayonnaise

½ cup sour cream

¼ cup fresh lemon juice

¼ cup snipped fresh dill

¾ tablespoon fresh pepper

Peel the cucumbers, cut them into pieces, and put in a colander. Toss with the salt and let stand 30 minutes to drain. Pat the cucumbers dry with paper towels.

By hand, chop the cucumbers on a cutting board into small pieces and put in a bowl. (Do not use a food processor; the cucumbers will turn to slush.) Add the remaining ingredients and stir until well blended. Transfer the sauce to an airtight container and chill.

This is especially appealing when served in a glass bowl.

APPLESAUCE

MAKES ABOUT 4 CUPS

10 medium McIntosh apples,
    peeled, cored, and sliced

1 cup water

1 cup sugar

Juice of ½ lemon

1 cinnamon stick (about
    3 inches long)

I make this applesauce to serve with a traditional Friday night dinner of chicken soup, chopped liver, and brisket. You can't imagine how good it tastes, because it too is traditional—made with just McIntosh apples (my longtime favorite), sugar, cinnamon, fresh lemon juice, and water. I like it chunky, the way applesauce used to be.

Of course, you must also have this on Chanukah to serve with the Potato Pancakes (page 141). For a complete Chanukah menu, see page 243.

In a large saucepan, combine all of the ingredients over medium heat. Bring to a gentle boil, then simmer, stirring occasionally, about 40 minutes, until the apple slices have softened but are not completely collapsed.

Pour the applesauce into a bowl, remove the cinnamon stick, and let cool. When cool, cover with plastic wrap and chill. Serve chilled.

Tomato Sauce

MAKES 5 TO 6 CUPS

This tomato sauce recipe was actually my husband's. Marvin gave it to our youngest daughter, Dena, who in turn passed it along to me. Nothing like keeping it in the family!

Unlike some other marinara sauces, you need only one hour to make this. I call for it in Stuffed Peppers (page 81) and Meat Loaf (page 79). Easy as it is to cook up a batch, I like to freeze it to have it on hand, and I suggest you do so, too.

Cover the bottom of a large sauté pan (11- or 12-inch) with olive oil, and heat over medium-high heat until hot but not smoking. Add the onion, and cook, stirring, until translucent, about 6 minutes. Stir in the tomatoes, reduce the heat to medium-low, and simmer, stirring occasionally, for 45 minutes.

While the tomatoes cook, pour enough olive oil into a small skillet to glaze the bottom of the pan. Add the garlic, basil, parsley, and oregano and cook over low heat, stirring, until the garlic is softened and only lightly colored.

When the tomatoes have cooked 45 minutes, stir the garlic-herb mixture into the tomato sauce in the sauté pan. Reduce the heat to low, and cook about 15 minutes. Taste and add salt and pepper, if desired.

Olive oil as needed

1 onion, finely chopped

2 cans (28 ounces each) crushed tomatoes

2 large garlic cloves, finely chopped

3 large basil leaves, finely chopped

Generous pinch chopped fresh parsley

Pinch dried oregano

Coarse kosher salt and fresh pepper, to taste

Use the sauce immediately, or let it cool and store in airtight containers in the refrigerator for up to 4 days or freeze for up to 1 month.

CRANBERRY-FIG CHUTNEY

MAKES 5½ CUPS

This is the chutney I make with my daughter Renée when we give cooking classes for Thanksgiving. It fits perfectly into a Succoth menu, as well, and is universally loved.

Note: If you make it at other times of the year, not fall or early winter, remember that fresh cranberries can be hard to find and may take some looking and/or special ordering.

❖

After you have removed the zest from the oranges, cut off the peels, discard, and cut the oranges into small pieces.

Combine the orange zest and segments and all the remaining ingredients in a large, heavy saucepan over medium-high heat, stirring occasionally, until the sugar dissolves, 8 to 10 minutes. Increase the heat to high and boil rapidly, stirring more frequently, for 20 to 30 minutes, until the cranberries pop and the mixture cooks down to a relish- or jamlike consistency. Remove the pan from the heat and let cool. (The chutney will thicken as it cools.)

Serve the chutney at room temperature.

The chutney will keep in an airtight container in the refrigerator for 1 week.

Grated zest of 2 medium oranges
2 bags (12 ounces each) fresh cranberries, rinsed, drained, and picked over
8 dried figs, chopped
½ cup finely chopped onion (1 small)
¼ cup raisins
3 cups sugar
3 tablespoons finely chopped peeled fresh ginger
1 teaspoon coarse kosher salt
1 teaspoon ground cinnamon
1 teaspoon cayenne pepper
1 teaspoon dry mustard

SAGE AND ROSEMARY RUB

MAKES ABOUT ¼ CUP

½ cup fresh roughly chopped
    sage leaves
½ cup fresh rosemary, the
    cluster of leaves only, no
    woody stem
8 garlic cloves, peeled
1 tablespoon coarse kosher salt

The more flavor you can give to poultry before roasting it, the better, and this rub does just that. I like the combination of fresh sage and rosemary on turkey in particular (see page 115), but there is no reason not to try it—sparingly, on account of the salt—on chicken as well.

In a small food processor, combine the sage leaves, rosemary, garlic, and salt, and process until chopped and well combined, but not pureed. Or chop very fine by hand. Use at once, or the herbs will turn black.

GARLIC OIL

MAKES ABOUT ¼ CUP

Up to twenty cloves of garlic may seem like an enormous amount—it is a lot—but I use this oil for seasoning meat and poultry. There is nothing timid about it. Making the oil fresh each time is best because the garlic will be at full strength, the way you want it.

For a small roasting chicken or hen, simply halve the recipe.

¼ cup olive oil

15 to 20 garlic cloves, minced

❖

In a small jar, combine the oil and garlic. Cover with a tight-fitting lid and store in the refrigerator for no more than 2 days.

TASTING MENUS

MENUS FOR EVERY DAY

FRIDAY NIGHT DINNER FOR MY FAMILY

The occasion was a Friday night dinner for my children and their spouses: Philip and Mara, Stuart and Julie, Laura and Quintus, Renée and Peter, Dena and Scott.

I was certain I had enough food for the crowd. We had a wonderful time, but I was amazed that there was not one crumb of anything left. Not a crumb.

"I guess you didn't make enough food," Dena remarked teasingly, getting up from the table.

"I guess I didn't," I replied, eying the empty platters and bowls.

I am still in shock!

Green Salad with Ginger Dressing
Chopped Liver
Challah

Lemon Chicken
Orange-Glazed Chicken
Lentil and Rice Pilaf
Cauliflower with Toasted Crumbs

Grandma's Apple "Cake"
Fresh Fruit

Coffee and Iced Tea

FRIDAY NIGHT DINNER FOR FRIENDS

Chopped Herring Salad

Apricot-Stuffed Chicken Breasts
Risi Bisi (Rice and Peas)
Cinnamon-Scented Salad

Delicious Chocolate Confection
(without the Chocolate Cream)
Fresh Strawberry Sauce

Coffee

A Birthday Celebration

Vegetable Soup

Shell Steak with Onions
Potato Dumplings
The Perfect Green Bean Salad
Grüne Salat (Green Salad with Sweet Dressing)

Apricot and Chocolate Tart
Prunes in White Wine

Coffee
Iced Tea with Lemon and Mint

An Anniversary Celebration

Romaine and Cucumber Salad with
Radishes and Tomatoes

Veal Stew with Mushrooms
Bow-Ties with Toasted Crumbs

or

Beef Goulash with Carrots and Potatoes
Pea Salad

Grandma's Apple "Cake"

Iced Tea
Coffee

A Dinner Party for Six

Pepper Ragout with Sausage
or
Wiener Schnitzel (Viennese Veal Cutlets)
Parsleyed Potatoes
Savoy Cabbage with Toasted Crumbs

Cucumber Salad
Sliced Beet Salad

Italian Plum Tart

Coffee

A Special Occasion Dinner

Veal Stew with Tomatoes and Green Pepper
Grüne Salat (Green Salad with Sweet Dressing)
Parsleyed Potatoes

Prunes in White Wine
Hazelnut Torte
Fresh Strawberry Sauce

Coffee

An Everyday Dinner

Tomato, Red Onion, Cucumber, and Parsley Salad

Fleischlabel (Chopped Meat Patties)
Kartoffelpuree (Mashed Potatoes)

Fresh Fruit
Homemade Cookies

Lemonade or Iced Tea

ANOTHER EVERYDAY DINNER

Beef Broth with Farina Dumplings

Flanken with Vegetables
Apple-Horseradish Sauce

Grüne Salat (Green Salad with Sweet Dressing)

A Selection of Homemade Cookies

Coffee

MENUS FOR JEWISH HOLIDAYS

A PASSOVER MENU

Chopped Liver
Matzo
Gefilte Fish
Apple-Horseradish Sauce

Chicken Soup with Matzo Balls

Brisket
Applesauce
Tomato, Red Onion, Cucumber, and Parsley Salad
Boiled Chicken with Soup Vegetables

Hazelnut Torte
Fresh Strawberry Sauce

Coffee

ROSH HASHANAH DINNER

Veal Roast with Roasted Fresh Vegetables
Brown Rice with Mushrooms
Endive and Red and Golden Beet Salad
with Scallion Dressing

Apple Bundt Cake

Iced Tea
Coffee

Rosh Hashanah dinner.

ROSH HASHANAH LUNCHEON

Green Salad with Ginger Dressing

Cholent

Strawberries and Blueberries

Tea

YOM KIPPUR NIGHT DINNER

Chicken Soup with Matzo Balls

Roast Chicken with Bread Stuffing

Peas and Carrots with White Sauce

Romaine and Cucumber Salad with Radishes
and Tomatoes

Grandma's Apple "Cake"

Beverage of Choice

A Menu for Shavuous

Your Preferred Liptauer
with
Black Bread, Unsalted Butter,
Sliced Radishes, Chopped Scallions, and
Chopped Chives
Deviled Eggs

Borscht

Fresh Salmon Cakes
or
Fried Flounder
Cucumber-Dill Sauce
Light Potato Salad
Cauliflower with Toasted Crumbs

◆

Marillenknadel (Fresh Apricot Dumplings)
Grandmother's Cheesecake

◆

Coffee

Shavuous Offerings, Savory and Sweet

Deviled Eggs (or plain hard-boiled eggs)

Liptauer (Fancy)

Liptauer with Anchovies

Liptauer with (More) Anchovies

My Most Favorite "Liptauer"

with

Black Bread and/or Challah

Unsalted Butter, Sliced Radishes, Chopped Scallions,

and Chopped Chives

and

Old-Fashioned Pound Cake

with Fresh Strawberry Sauce and *Schlag*

Chocolate Streusel Bundt Cake

Grandma's Cheesecake

Delicious Chocolate Confection with Chocolate Cream

Crepes with Cream Cheese Filling and Apricot Sauce

Butter Horns and Cinnamon Twists

Coffee with *Schlag*

Succoth Dinner
(or a Thanksgiving Menu)

Eggs with Sautéed Onions

Black Bread

Chopped Salad

Roast Turkey with Apple, Almond, and Raisin Stuffing

Cranberry-Fig Chutney

Barley Pilaf with Shiitake Mushrooms and Onions

Tzimmes

Peas and Carrots with White Sauce

Corn Bread

Harvest "Cake"

Coffee

A Chanukah Dinner

Potato Pancakes
Applesauce

Backhendl (Fried Chicken, Viennese Style)
Cucumber Salad

Italian Plum Tart

Tea or Coffee

Index

Page references in italics indicate photographs.